FOOTBALL
FOOTBALL
RIVALS

MANCHESTER
UNITED
VS
MANCHESTER
CITY

Classic
MANCHESTER
Derby Games

David Clayton

Dedication:

For Callum, Leah, Ian and Claire Howarth.
And also for Pablo Zabaleta.
They all know the reasons why...
And also for Dave and Mike Wilson – born wearing
red-tinted glasses...

CONTENTS

Introduction

The Teams Who Love to Hate One Another

City vs United, United vs City – whichever way you like to call it, there is no game quite like the Manchester derby. The passion, the atmosphere, the blood-and-thunder tackles and the fear that, for the next few months at least, one set of fans will have to go into hiding while the other set seem to win the city for a time.

The Manchester derby has a long proud tradition that stretches way, way back into the dim and distant past – but how and when did the rivalry become fierce to the point of hatred? This book traces the earliest origins of this fixture back to the very beginning and sources the incidents, games and actions that gradually drove a wedge between these two proud clubs.

Theories are offered on why United currently command bigger crowds – though for many years it was City who were the better supported of the two clubs – and looks at the pivotal moments that changed football in Manchester forever.

The scandals, the controversy, the back-biting, jealousy and mind games – no stone is left unturned in a bid to delve deeper into the psyche of these two proud teams and their legions of followers.

Yet, despite the hostilities, when the chips have been down at either club, the other has offered a helping hand, and after the Second World War and the Munich air disaster, City and United, for a time, were a footballing city united in every sense. Whisper it, but the underlying thread throughout this book is that there really is a love-hate relationship between the Reds and the Blues.

Imagine if either City or United didn't exist. Each set of fans would probably celebrate till the early hours at the enemy's demise. But in the days that followed, I guarantee there would be a longing for the old days when each club was going at the other hammer and tongs. In short, one would miss the other and the banter that goes with this much-loved fixture. Sounds far-fetched?

There has been pain while one watches the other enjoy glory years and it's happened to both sets of fans, as history will show. In the modern era, it's been particularly painful for City and the loyal thousands who have stuck with them, as one comedian once commented, through thin and thin. Yet we only need look at the 2011/12 season, where the eyes of the world were on Manchester, as the most intriguing title race took one twist after another and the Blues finally ended 44 years of pain by winning the Premier League. United's reign of being top dogs in the city finally came to an end, and City fans will hope they can enjoy an equal amount of time in the sun – but United will not lie down.

The future of football in Manchester is bright and the duel between City and United has never been more fascinating.

Yes, we all love and dread derby day in equal measure, but it's still the first game both City and United fans look for when the FA releases the new season's fixture list – no matter what either side might say. Long may that continue.

David Clayton, Manchester, 2012

"I shall be working hard from now until Wednesday on making the side against United. I'll even play without wages and on crutches, if they'll let me."

Mike Doyle, *Daily Mirror*, 1971

Early Kick-off

1881–1899

"In no previous seasons, it may truly be asserted, has the meeting of two local rivals been looked forward to with such a great amount of interest in Manchester football circles."

The Umpire, January 1895

Supporters of Manchester City will tell you they are the people's club of Manchester, and tracing the club's humble beginnings it's hard to argue against those claims. Manchester United fans, however, will tell you their club was formed two years before the Blues and therefore they are the original godfathers of Mancunian football. The arguments in this story begin early!

For City, the origins of its existence were both noble and, in some instances, life-changing as members of St Mark's Church of England in West Gorton originally founded the football club for humanitarian purposes more than anything else.

In 1865, Gorton had welcomed the new church that had been built as it provided a much-needed focal point for a community with very little else going for it. The new reverend, Arthur Connell, and his daughter Anna would make a lasting impression on Manchester and arrived determined to help the people of the area by being both innovative and forward-thinking in their approach. Arthur and Anna were desperate to help members of their parish, who were trapped in a world of drink-fuelled violence, poverty and unemployment. They needed something else to fill the voids in their lives and, if religion wasn't the answer, perhaps there was something else?

In particular, it was Anna who believed some form of social activity could harness the male population of the community, and it didn't take her long to come to the conclusion that football, becoming more and more a sport that was popular within the poorer areas of Manchester and the country as a whole, was an ideal solution.

Alcoholism and gang violence plagued large areas of East Manchester, with Gorton one of the worst hit areas, and while another member of the church, warden William Beastow, had successfully run a community cricket club in the summer months since 1875, there was little else to do in the long Mancunian winters in a sporting sense.

The Connells believed their idea could work and they visited all areas of their parish, both Catholic and Protestant, in a bid to get their football team up and running.

Men of all backgrounds and religions were invited to join and, when enough interest had been registered, Beastow and fellow warden Thomas Goodbehere finally formed a team. In 1880, St Mark's of West Gorton began playing their football on an area of rough ground adjacent to Clowes Street – technically the fledgling club's first home.

The first recorded match was on 13th November 1880 and saw St Mark's suffer a 2-1 defeat to a team called Baptist Church of Macclesfield – and both teams played with 12 players. The shirts worn by St Mark's were black with white shorts and a Maltese cross on their breast – though the reasons behind this are unknown. A year later, the name was changed to West Gorton (St Mark's) and, three years after that, they became Gorton, as the connection to the church grew evermore tenuous. The club's name, players and officials changed regularly around this time and in 1887 the new identity was Ardwick FC, with the team now playing at its fifth ground. It was around this time that an ideal venue was discovered for a home ground and Hyde Road became the destination for the supporters of one of the embryonic Manchester clubs to flock to.

Not too far away and prior to the founding of St Mark's, Lancashire and Yorkshire Railway workers in Newton Heath formed two football teams as early as 1878. Newton Heath Loco represented workers from the Motive Power Division, while Newton Heath LYR represented members of the Carriage and Wagon department. The team began life in an organized and steady manner, with funding from the wealthy railway company owners and a home ground on North Road. It is difficult to pinpoint when the club really got on its tracks but, during 1882/83, Newton Heath LYR played 23 recorded friendlies, and the first official game was recorded in the Lancashire Cup in 1883/84. By 1890 the club was no longer sponsored by the railway, though many of their players were still employed by the company. In 1892 they would change their name to Newton Heath, dropping the LYR altogether, and in 1893, "the Heathens" moved to a new ground at Bank Street in Clayton – some 110 years later, Manchester City would move to a new stadium just a couple of miles away.

The first Manchester derby on record would be unrecognizable to the supporters of the two Premier League giants of today. Yet, when West Gorton (St Mark's) took on Newton Heath LYR on 12th November 1881, it began a city rivalry that would eventually divide Manchester into two halves: one red, one blue.

Both fledgling clubs were in their infancy and would go through numerous changes, play at several venues and even change their colours, before each adopted the name of the city they played in as a common denominator that would make Manchester, Bristol, Sheffield and Glasgow unique on derby days. Of those titanic tussles there is only one City vs United, however – something Mancunians are fiercely proud of, though neither side would admit as much.

"A pleasant game" is how that first meeting was reported as being in the *Ashton Reporter*, probably one of the few clashes between the clubs during a rivalry that stretches back more than 131 years that could be described as such, and the Heathens, who initially played in scarlet and black, triumphed 3-0 to set the ball rolling.

Football was still in its infancy, but as many as 3,000 people – most curious bystanders – watched the game, which had no real significance other than a first recorded meeting. As the sport grew in popularity, so the matches became more common, but with only the FA Cup a nationally recognized competition at that time and no league until 1888, the Manchester Cup became the competition in which the sides met on a regular basis.

With West Gorton dropping St Mark's, then "West" from their name Gorton eventually became Ardwick FC in 1887 as the club went through a number of Manchester suburbs seeking a place they could call home.

Newton Heath were considered the stronger of the two teams but their attempts to join the Football League, formed in 1888, were initially thwarted as the election process denied them the opportunity to join the elite band of founder league members until 1892 when the Heathens were elected to the First Division and Ardwick to the Second. It was a momentous time for Manchester football, though one half of the city felt understandably slighted all the same.

Prior to this, and frustrated at the Football Association's reluctance to admit them, Newton Heath and Ardwick joined a rival organization, the Football Alliance, and met twice during the 1891/92 season, with Newton Heath now wearing red and white quarter-coloured shirts, winning 3-1 on their own ground. The return fixture ended 2-2 in front of an estimated 10,000 crowd. Interest was clearly growing! Almost 1,000 more had attended when the teams met in the FA Cup first qualifying-round clash – arguably the first official meeting – which Newton Heath again won, this time by 5-1. Ardwick had, by this point, adopted light blue as their colours, ditching their previous dark colours once and for all (and possibly because they clashed with the Heathens' red and white).

Perhaps the willingness to challenge the FA paved a way for the Manchester clubs to finally win election – it certainly seemed to speed up the process! The fact both clubs were in separate divisions meant no meetings for the next couple of seasons and, as Ardwick Football Club ceased to be in 1894, in effect going out of business, a new club, Manchester City, rose from the ashes like a phoenix from the flames and took their place.

City had been the first to take on Manchester in its name and by the time the first league derby occurred in 1894 it was Manchester City vs Newton Heath – a game played in Division Two following Newton Heath's relegation and played at City's Hyde Road ground, former home of the now defunct Ardwick. It's worth noting that the Heathens decided to adopt green and gold quartered shirts in 1894, though they would return to red two years later. Interestingly, when future generations of the club's supporters protested against their American owners, it would be to the green and gold colours they turned to as a symbol of their stand.

As far as the rest of the country was concerned, this was THE first official meeting between the Manchester clubs, and an expectant 14,000 crowd gathered to see if City could finally get one over on their rivals. The teams went into the game on level points, but City trailed Newton Heath by four places and had played four games more. City had scored 30 goals in 11 games but conceded the same amount, while Heath had lost just one of their seven matches and again started as favourites.

Befitting a Manchester derby, leaden skies greeted the teams as play began, but the sun did appear partway through the match – though this was the only bright spot for the hosts who, despite having debutant Billy Meredith in their ranks, were again soundly beaten on their own patch, losing 5-2.

Meredith, at least, proved a revelation. The winger had been spotted by City director Lawrence Furniss, who saw the Welsh forward in action for Northwich Victoria. In fact, Furniss had a privileged view, being the referee on that particular occasion!

Furniss and another City official travelled to Meredith's home village in Chirk, North Wales, where they were met with suspicion and, initially, anger from locals who weren't used to seeing "outsiders". A few jugs of beer seemed to calm the protestations and a meeting was finally arranged, but Meredith's mother issued a warning when she told the City officials: "It is all very well for you gentlemen to leave your big cities and come to our villages to steal our boys away... our boys are happy and healthy, satisfied with their work and innocent amusements... if Billy takes my advice he will stick to his work and play football for his own amusement when work is finished."

Meredith had recently started as an employee at the Black Park colliery as a pit pony driver, but football was in his blood and he was eventually convinced to join the Blues, a move that would change his life forever as well as putting his tiny village on the map. Meredith did his own thing and was a character on and off the pitch, invariably cycling from Chirk to Manchester from training and matches in the early years of his career, at least so legend tells us.

His debut saw City lose defender Harry Smith and go down to 10 men (with substitutes still a long way off being incorporated) and, though Meredith made a sparkling start with two goals on his bow, it was inside-left Richard Smith who stole the show as he scored four times in a comprehensive win for the Heathens. For this landmark first official derby it's worth recording the two teams of the day – City lined up: George Hutchison, Harry Smith, John Walker, George Mann, Joseph Nash, Fred Dyer, Billy Meredith, Pat Finnerhan, Sandy Rowan, James Sharples and Bob Milarvie. Newton Heath's XI was: William Douglas, John McCartney, Fred Erentz, George Perrins, James McNaught, William Davidson, John Clarkin, Robert Donaldson, James Dow, Richard Smith and James Peters – each and every man a pioneer in their own right.

City's reputation for unpredictability stretches all the way back to their first season in the Football League, and their form going into the return derby at Clayton underlined perfectly that early inconsistency, having beaten Woolwich Arsenal 4-1 one week and then lost 8-0 away to Burton just 11 days later.

By contrast, Newton Heath were steady and heading for promotion having lost just three of their 19 games to that point – and none of them were at Clayton, though a recent 3-0 loss at Lincoln suggested there were still one or two chinks in their armoury. As it was, the game produced few surprises and, after John Clarkin put the home side ahead on seven minutes, the result was never really in doubt. More than 12,000 watched the Heathens complete the match in emphatic style, winning 4-1 – though it's worth noting the visitors were actually far better than the scoreline suggests. It was a foreboding start for City, however, to have already suffered a league double defeat to their neighbours as each team battled for early supremacy in the city.

The match had created quite a buzz and was now eagerly anticipated by both sets of supporters; the early Manchester derby was indeed finally up and running, even if it had proved a little one-sided. The five meetings to date had seen Newton Heath rack up four wins and 19 goals compared with City's one draw and seven goals. What the derby needed was a little more parity and a City win to stoke up the occasion but, on the evidence seen to date, that was still a way off.

The Heathens had a chance to win promotion at the end of the 1894/95 campaign with a third-place finish winning them a Test Match – a forerunner of the play-offs – and a chance for the promotion they so desperately craved. But it wasn't to be and a 3-0 defeat to Stoke City ensured the derby was on the fixture list again the following season.

Dubbed "the championship of Cottonopolis", the Manchester

derby was the first game both sets of fans looked for when the 1895/96 fixtures were released in the Press. The third league derby also saw the clubs enter the contest on a far more level playing field, following City's fine start of four wins in their first five games, and for the Clayton derby it was the visitors who were in the ascendancy in third, though Newton Heath were just a point and one position behind.

The build-up to the game had convinced the Heathens to provide extra space for the larger-than-usual expected crowd, but a torrential downpour meant much of it went unused, with just under 12,000 braving the elements by kick-off. In the mud-bath resembling a football pitch, City soon showed why they were already pushing for promotion with a dominant first-half display, but a rather fortuitous goal for the hosts broke the deadlock, with the conditions playing their part, and when Charlie Williams misjudged a low cross by Clarkin and the ball somehow found its way into the back of the net. It was harsh on the visitors but, on 55 minutes, a sweeping move saw Sandy Rowan level the scores – the question was, could City now go on and record that elusive first derby win? Though their overall performance probably merited both points, City had keeper Williams to thank for avoiding a galling 90th-minute defeat after he produced a superb save as the Heathens put on a grandstand finish and defender David Robson held his head in his hands as the City keeper kept out his thunderbolt shot from close range. A 1-1 draw at least ensured both Manchester clubs' promotion hopes remained intact, even so early in the campaign.

The teams met again just two months later and City's long wait for a win over their neighbours finally came to an end. Going into the match as the division's leaders, the hosts were determined to give the packed Hyde Road crowd what the majority of them had come along for – a home win. Yet more adverse weather – a regular staple of the early fixtures – didn't deter 18,000 people attending the eagerly awaited match, and there was a good sprinkling of Newton

Heath fans among the throngs of people. What was also becoming clear was that football was the sport of the working class and that Manchester was already in love with it.

Already, in the factories across the city, divisions were being formed and the question asked – are you City or Newton Heath? Followers of either club were anticipating and dreading the fallout of a derby game and the banter that would inevitably follow.

The fourth league derby didn't disappoint the capacity crowd, with both teams committed to attacking whenever the opportunity arose. The brilliant Billy Meredith, the first real star of Manchester football, was the biggest threat to the Heathens' unbeaten derby record, and it was the Welsh Wizard who inevitably laid on City's opener with just four minutes played when Robert Hill emphatically tucked home his teasing cross.

Despite being outplayed and, at times, having to cling on, the Heathens showed their resilience by levelling through Joe Cassidy and then having the opportunity to go into the break with an unlikely lead following a first-ever derby penalty, but it was squandered and it would prove a costly miss.

After the break, the brilliance of Meredith proved to be the difference on the day as he produced a trademark mesmeric dribble to see off Walter Cartwright and Erentz before beating Newton keeper Douglas with a fierce shot. Despite a frantic finish that goal proved to be the winner, and it was fitting that the man of the match – arguably the most popular footballer in world football (such as it was at the time!) – should settle the affair and give City fans that long-awaited first win. Gate receipts were totted up to be a not insubstantial £410, proving there was money to be made in football.

Yet, just as the Heathens had done the year before, City were denied promotion by the cruellest of circumstances, finishing second and level on points with Liverpool but with an inferior goal average. The fact the Merseysiders had scored 106 goals compared with the

Blues' 63 suggests they were perhaps worthy winners.

Crowds for the derby were getting progressively larger and an estimated 20,000 witnessed the 1896/97 Hyde Road clash that was yet again blighted by heavy rain – no wonder Manchester had earned the nickname "the Rainy City" – but on this occasion there were no goals to warm the dampened masses as the normally goal-laden match ended 0-0.

The return was played before a capacity 18,000 crowd and a tired-looking City went down 2-1 with the heavy going affecting the Blues' superior passing game. In the battle that commenced the Heathens adapted better and, in reality, won far more comfortably than the score suggests. This encounter proved one thing: neither Clayton nor Hyde Road were truly capable of housing the crowds that now demanded to see these games. The match was stopped a number of times, for crowd encroachment, with former City boss Joshua Parlby, now a member of the League Management Committee, warning the home fans that their club would face the consequences should the game be abandoned. Smith and Donaldson scored for the home side, with Hill's goal for City no more than a consolation when order was finally restored.

Ultimately, Newton Heath missed out again on promotion after finishing second and losing to Sunderland over two games in the increasingly dreaded Test Match. The Blues finished a disappointing sixth as their bid to escape the confines of Division Two failed yet again.

By 1897/98, the Blues again looked serious promotion candidates as they arrived at Clayton having won all seven of their games and looking more sharp and confident than ever before. The Heathens, yet again, proved stubborn opponents and proved that, even at this early stage, the formbook was thrown away prior to derby day.

In fact, Matthew Gillespie's goal seemed to have earned the Reds two welcome points in front of Clayton's biggest gate yet – 20,000

– but defender Dick Ray charged down field in the last minute to whip a spectacular shot past Frank Barrett and into the top corner to preserve his side's unbeaten start and to earn City what had looked like an unlikely 1-1 draw. The Christmas Day return derby at Hyde also hinted that the Reds were back in control of proceedings, with Joe Cassidy's solitary strike ruining many a festive period in the blue half of Manchester. In fact, City's second loss of the season would have a devastating effect on the second-placed Blues who would win just five of their remaining 17 games to finish third.

That Manchester led the world in many areas yet failed to have either of its two most prominent clubs in the top division was a source of frustration for all Mancunians, yet the Heathens' 3-0 win at Clayton suggested, at last, they might go and take the division by storm. A brace from Cassidy – including the first converted penalty – and another from the prolific Hugh Boyd put the Reds top, but the Blues responded magnificently to the set-back and, by the time the Boxing Day return kicked off, topped the table, inspired by the brilliant Meredith who had bagged 15 goals in 16 matches. Fred Williams cheered the capacity 25,000 crowd with a goal before the break and Meredith doubled City's lead after the break. A controversial third followed when Gillespie bundled Reds' keeper Frank Barrett into the net with the ball still in his hands – but the ref saw no foul and the goal stood – and George Dougal netted a fourth. It was only City's second win in 10 attempts but the emphatic margin suggested a power-shift between the Manchester clubs and the Blues never looked back, winning their first title and at last winning promotion to Division One. When the teams next met it truly was a Manchester derby in every sense, but for now the Reds would have to watch their neighbours claim undisputed bragging rights for the immediate future. It would be four years before Manchester next saw its two giants go into battle, and by then the anticipation had reached fever pitch...

Scandal!

1899–1910

"Though rollercoasters had not yet been invented, if they had the thought of them and Manchester City would surely have been linked forever."

While Newton Heath struggled to leave the confines of Division Two, City consolidated their first season in the top flight by finishing a respectable seventh in 1899/1900. Both Manchester clubs finished in mid-table in their respective divisions the season after, but the 1901/02 campaign was more disappointing still, with the Reds again floundering in the second tier and City relegated despite showing the form of champions in the second half of the campaign. Unfortunately, all the damage had been done in the first part of the campaign, where 13 defeats in the first 19 games left the Blues with too great a mountain to climb.

With Newton Heath almost going out of business in January 1902, Manchester United, now donning red shirts and white shorts, emerged from the debris and at last Manchester had two teams who bore the name of the city.

By Christmas 1902 the wait for supporters of both clubs was finally over with the first ever Manchester United vs Manchester City derby. United took on City in sky blue in front of a record derby crowd of 40,000 – the people of Manchester had spoken – this was now not only the highlight of the local sporting calendar but also a match that was capturing the imagination of the whole country.

A strong, blustery wind made conditions difficult, but Billy

Meredith was imperious, toothpick in the corner of his mouth as per usual, giving the Division Two leaders the edge after the break and the Blues also hit the woodwork, United, though, largely outplayed and fortunate to still be interested in the outcome, stole a late point when Ernest Pegg levelled on 70 minutes. Five minutes from the end Meredith tricked his way through, but his shot struck the bar and the Reds clung on for a 1-1 draw.

City powered on towards promotion thereafter, and a win in the return derby at Hyde would see the Blues crowned champions and rubberstamp an instant return to the top flight. More than 30,000 fans packed City's ground ready for a party but United hadn't read the script and were ahead in five minutes through an own goal by William Holmes. The goal knocked the stuffing out of the Blues and, when Alf Schofield doubled United's lead shortly after the restart of the second half, City's proud unbeaten home record was as good as over. The Blues battled on, but it just wasn't their day and the Reds comfortably hung on for a shock 2-0 win.

United's dominance in this fixture was a serious concern for City fans who had now seen just two victories in the first dozen meetings – at least they could console themselves with the Division Two title, confirmed with two more victories in the final two games.

The Blues went into the 1903/04 campaign on the crest of a wave and wrote their name into the history books in the process – but it could have been so much better. After securing the FA Cup with a 1-0 win over Bolton Wanderers at the Crystal Palace, City went into their final league game knowing a victory at third-placed Everton and defeat for leaders Sheffield Wednesday, who travelled to mid-table Derby, would complete an historic league and FA Cup double. Sadly, the Owls won and the Blues went down 1-0. Still, it was City who could rightly claim to be the first Manchester club to bring a major trophy back to the city. United narrowly missed out on promotion for what seemed the umpteenth time, finishing third and just two points behind Division Two champions Arsenal.

No derbies again, then, for the 1904/05 season, with United and City both finishing third in their respective divisions, but the Blues were about to be shamed by a match-fixing scandal that shook the whole of football.

City went into the final game against Aston Villa knowing that if Everton and Newcastle failed to win, the title was theirs. A 3-2 defeat at Villa Park was bad enough, but when allegations that Billy Meredith had offered Villa player Alex Leake £10 to lose the game emerged, City acted swiftly, knowing full well they were about to break up one of the best teams English football had seen up to that point.

The brilliant Meredith was handed an 18-month ban from playing and told his City career was over. The investigations uncovered irregularities and suspicious behaviour from a total of 17 players and club officials, including manager Tom Maley.

The Blues were effectively having to start from scratch all over again but, despite this, City put in a sterling effort during the 1905/06 season, eventually finishing third with only a poor run of results in the final few games preventing a first top-flight title. The Reds, meanwhile, had taken on five of City's best players in the fallout from the bribery scandal and had gone on to end their 11-year Division One exile by finishing runners-up to Bristol City.

United had also taken on the still-banned Billy Meredith – a hammer blow to City fans who had worshipped the ground he walked on – but with the ban remaining in place the Welsh Wizard would have to wait until the New Year to make his debut for the Reds.

In the meantime, there was still the small matter of a first top-division Manchester derby after a dozen meetings in Division Two. It was the only place these two giants of English football deserved to be and the city held its breath on 1st December 1906, when the two tribes finally went to war.

The Blues hosted the game, and with the biggest crowd yet in attendance – more than 40,000 – it was United who were expected to continue their dominance, with City enduring an awful first half of the season. Indeed, the Blues shipped 16 goals in their first three games of the campaign, losing 9-1 to Everton along the way, and looked relegation certainties, while United consolidated well after promotion.

With emotions running high in both camps, and a crowd bursting at the seams crammed into Hyde Road, it was City's turn to upset the form book with easily their best performance of the season. Billy Lot Jones put the Blues ahead on 20 minutes and George Stewart's deflected effort doubled the lead three minutes later; the same player sealed the points early in the second half after splitting the United defence and finishing with a clinical drive past Harry Moger to make it 3-0. The City fans carried keeper Walter Smith off as they celebrated a famous derby win.

Another huge crowd greeted the teams for the return at Clayton, with City fans having to swallow the bitter pill of seeing former idol Meredith spearhead the United attack for the first time, as well as former favourites Sandy Turnbull and Herbert Burgess also playing in red. With so much hyperbole surrounding the game it is perhaps not that surprising that the match didn't quite live up to its billing.

City took an early lead after Burgess – of all players – handled the ball in the box and George Dorsett made no mistake from the spot. Meredith was largely ineffective, though he did indirectly help United back into the game when he collided with City centre-half Bill Eadie just after the break and the Blues defender came off worse and was unable to continue. With no subs allowed, and City down to 10 men, the Reds eventually levelled through Charlie Roberts, though Jimmy Conlin's late goal for City appeared to have pinched a famous win only for the referee to rule it out for offside. Still, with three points from four, the bragging rights belonged to the Blues who extended their unbeaten run against their neighbours to five. It also justified their decision to do what was viewed as the right thing by kicking out those connected with the match-fixing scandal.

It was, however, the calm before the storm.

With the former City stars bedded in and forming the backbone of the team, United's ascendency quickly kicked in and the Blues were left wondering what might have been had the controversy never happened. It was particularly cruel for City, who had nurtured the precocious talents of Meredith and Turnbull, that the pair should become their chief tormentors, driven on either by a sense of injustice or plain old revenge.

The Blues had behaved impeccably throughout the whole sorry episode and had done the right thing, but at what cost?

The opportunity to dominate English football had apparently gone and, that the initiative had been handed to their city rivals was almost too much to bear for some followers, and, for the first time, the 15th league Manchester derby saw some of that ill feeling bubble to the surface.

A slick and ruthless United came into the game on 21st December 1907 having won 14 of their 17 games and topped the table comfortably – they were, in fact, steamrollering their way to the title. City were having a steady campaign and had lost just three of their 15 matches but the Reds, roared on by a crowd approaching 35,000, stormed into a 3-0 lead, with George Wall opening the scoring, before a fired-up Sandy Turnbull bagged two more to put the game out of the Blues' reach. Bill Eadie pulled one back, but the real fireworks were still to come as Turnbull was sent off for punching former team-mate George Dorsett near the end of the contest. It was the worst incident of a number of little niggles and it perhaps underlined the growing chasm between the two Manchester clubs, both on and off the pitch.

The return derby saw United arrive at a capacity Hyde Road already assured of an historic first Division One title, while City were still in with a chance of the runners-up spot. The Reds deserved no less after a sparkling season when, despite the controversy, they had let the football do the talking and reaped the rewards as a result.

The game was feisty, bad-tempered and littered with incidents that were fast becoming the trademark of the Manchester derby. The 0-0 draw meant the Blues would eventually finish third, but the derbies of the 1907/08 season had proved that the gloves were well and truly off between United and City. In fact things would never be the same again.

There was more pain for the Blues in the 1908/09 season with United completing the double, winning 2-1 at Hyde Road and 3-1 at Clayton. In the first meeting Irvine Thornley put the Blues deservedly ahead in the first half, but two slices of bad luck for City gifted United goals, with Jimmy Turnbull eventually profiting from a stumble by Tommy Kelso, and then an unfortunate collision from a Meredith cross gifted Harold Halse with the simplest of chances to take the points for the reigning champions. While City fans understandably bemoaned their luck, United fans equally claimed they had earned their good fortune by sheer persistence. The Clayton return saw City punished once again by a former old boy – this time George Livingstone – in a comfortable home win.

Livingstone marked his debut with two goals in the first 15 minutes and there was no way back for the Blues from there, with Wall making it three before Jimmy Conlin pulled back a late consolation. The atmosphere was as muted as anyone could remember, with neither side having particularly good league campaigns. At least United could console themselves with a second major trophy in two seasons as they beat Bristol City 1-0 in the FA Cup final to end the season on a high – and if they felt like being particularly mischievous, they could point to the fact that former City duo Billy Meredith and Sandy Turnbull had won the match for them – Meredith being voted man of the match, and Turnbull scoring the only goal. For the Blues, an erratic campaign that had begun by topping the table with an opening day win over Sunderland, ended by slipping into the relegation zone on the final day of the season. City now faced the prospect of Division Two football for the first time in seven years.

Fortunately, it was to be a short-lived experience as City went into the last game of the 1909/10 season knowing a point would clinch the second-tier title. However, a 3-2 defeat at Wolverhampton Wanderers meant an agonizing wait to see if Hull City had floundered against Oldham Athletic – they had, and the Blues were back in the top flight again. Though rollercoasters had not yet been invented, if they had the thought of them and Manchester City would surely have been linked forever.

The Next Level

1910–1919

"All future negotiations with United now and for the future are now closed."

Manchester City matchday programme, 1913

Manchester United's relocation from the crumbling Bank Street ground in Clayton to the salubrious surrounds of Old Trafford confirmed that the Reds were, probably, the richest and most ambitious club in the land. Backed by wealthy owner John Henry Davies, £60,000 was spent constructing the 80,000-capacity stadium near the Bridgewater Canal, and by the start of the 1910/11 season the new ground was ready for United to call their home. It also led to the nickname "Moneybags United" and highlighted further the direction the two clubs appeared to be taking. If ambition was a crime, the Reds were guilty as charged. As it was, they had an owner who was determined to make the club a major force in English football and lay the foundations of a football dynasty.

How City would have loved to leave Hyde Road and move to a swanky new stadium themselves. But this was still more than a decade away from becoming reality. Instead, £3,000 was spent covering three sides of the ground that often saw its spectators head home sodden wet having had no protection from the elements.

United had also flexed their financial muscle in the transfer market purchasing prolific Nottingham Forest striker Enoch "Knocker" West for a not insubstantial £850 fee. It was yet another statement of intent by the Reds who were only too happy to demonstrate their financial muscle when needed.

The first Old Trafford derby was a special occasion for all concerned and United were determined not to taste defeat in their new surrounds. A crowd of more than 60,000 gathered to see the city rivals resume their battle for bragging rights – a new record that smashed the previous best of 40,000 by 20,000 – and with City determined not to be the bridesmaids, a feisty match ensued.

The Reds drew first blood, with West and Sandy Turnbull putting the hosts 2-0 up with 37 minutes on the clock. Jones made amends after the break by reducing the arrears, but it was too little too late.

By the time the teams met again at Hyde Road, City were 14 points behind United, who were pressing for their second title in four years, as Meredith and Turnbull continued on their mission to make their former employers suffer. But, as ever, form meant little going into the Manchester derby. Lot Jones put the Blues ahead in the first half after fine work by George Stewart and David Ross presented the Welshman with a simple tap-in to send the majority of the 40,000 crowd into raptures. In fact, there may have been even more in attendance, such was the clamour to see the game, and several fans were injured in the cramped and tightly-packed throngs.

Yet again, though, City hearts were broken by two old boys as Meredith supplied the cross that Sandy Turnbull gleefully converted to earn United a 1-1 draw – a valuable point as it turned out, with the Reds winning the title by a solitary point, while the Blues finished just four points ahead of second bottom Bristol City.

Neither Manchester club had a particularly fruitful 1911/12 season. United tamely surrendered their title, while City seemed happy to retain their top-flight status, and the two derbies produced 0-0 stalemates. The Reds would end a disappointing campaign just two points ahead of the Blues in mid-table.

If City fans still felt aggrieved at the way they had lost some of their best players to United, the 1912/13 season was about to see some payback.

George Wynn scored the goal that gave City their first ever win at Old Trafford, with the 1-0 victory also meaning the Reds had failed to score against City for three successive games. The goal sparked wild celebrations among the City contingent in the 38,911 crowd but, two days later, there was even more to celebrate as double title-winning United manager Ernest Mangnall left Old Trafford to take over the reins at City – the move shook Manchester football to the core. The question was could Mangnall replicate his success in the blue half of the city?

The answer, at least immediately, was no, as just four months later United returned to winning ways on derby day with an impressive 2-0 victory at Hyde Road. The now standard mud-bath of a pitch greeted both sets of players, and, yet again, Meredith was at the heart of United's best moments including laying on Enoch West's second of the game on 23 minutes to complete the scoring.

The Reds would finish fourth and City sixth as neither Manchester club disgraced themselves following a steady, if not spectacular, campaign.

With just five goals in the previous five derbies it seemed the occasion was getting the better of the players as time went by. The Blues were, in particular, finding scoring a problem with a total of just seven goals in the previous 11 derbies, and that statistic would not improve much over the next two seasons. The December 1913 Hyde Road meeting again saw United triumph 2-0, with George Anderson on target twice to condemn City to yet another demoralizing defeat. The simmering ill feeling between the two rivals continued unabated as well, with the matchday programme referring to a possible transfer of a fringe City player to the Reds with the line "all future negotiations with United now and for the future are now closed." It seemed the animosity now ran very deep indeed, with some factions of the City hierarchy and the supporters unable to stomach the fact that Meredith and Turnbull went from heroes to zeroes by switching Mancunian allegiances even several years on. United had little to complain about as they'd been in a win-win situation from the word go – the heart of a very good City side ripped out and now playing in red shirts was enough, but clearly Meredith, Turnbull and company felt they'd been poorly treated and had a burning desire to rub their former employers' noses in the dirt. The truth of the scandal, however, would never really be known.

City's goal drought in this fixture – and in general – had seen them splash out £1,780 on Tommy Browell, and the Blues' form after the latest derby set-back took an upward turn, though Mangnall's side was infuriatingly inconsistent, with winning sequences followed by losing runs. City had, however, done enough to go into the 26th Manchester derby at Old Trafford knowing a victory would give them an excellent chance of finishing higher than their neighbours for the first time in 11 years – and when James Cumming struck the only goal to give City a 1-0 win, that's exactly how things transpired. Though the bunting was kept in the cupboards and the open-top carriages left in the garages, the Blues' 13th-place finish was one higher than the Reds, who had a marginally worse goal average. Still, it was the first time since Meredith and Turnbull had been kicked out that City had finished in the ascendency.

The 1914/15 derby at United was the seventh successive meeting between the clubs where the home team had failed to score, and the 0-0 draw at Old Trafford meant City hadn't conceded a goal away to the Reds for almost seven hours in total – 413 minutes all told – an incredible record stretching back four years. But this game was played despite the First World War breaking out, and there were doubts whether the season would even be completed.

The *Manchester Guardian* reported that City had released a statement saying: "If any professional in our pay wishes to serve his King, we will do our best for his dependents provided we have any money taken at the gates."

The 20,000 Old Trafford crowd was also a new low, illustrating the concerns of the ordinary man on the street and the place football occupied in peoples' lives at that moment in time.

The teams met at Hyde Road once more before the league programme was indefinitely suspended, and a 1-1 draw brought an end to local rivalry for a while. United had taken a first-half lead through Knocker West, but the Blues levelled when Fred Howard – who had missed a penalty before the break – hit a low drive through a forest of legs and past Robert Beale for a deserved equalizer.

The teams headed into the enforced break with City again top dogs in Manchester, having finished in fifth, while the Reds escaped relegation by one point. The Reds' ageing side was on the decline, and even the great Meredith was on the decline, though he still had one last hurrah to come when the league programme resumed...

Blues Fight Back

1919–1923

"Meredith had the scribes drooling as he turned back the clock to his heyday with a stunning performance – and to think he'd played in virtually every Manchester derby since 1894 in either a blue or a red shirt…"

Though City and United met 16 times during the First World War, the matches were in regional divisions and subsidiary tournaments meant to keep the clubs ticking along until league action resumed. A mixture of players represented each Manchester club, some by invitation; others were regular squad members not involved with the armed forces. Billy Meredith played many times for City, perhaps indicating that he'd never really wanted to leave the Blues in the first place and that time had healed wounds on both sides.

By the time the conflict had ended and the Division One programme resumed City began almost where they'd left off with Tommy Broad, signed from Bristol City, the only new addition. By contrast, United had invested in an entirely new side and, for the derby on 11th October 1919, no players remained from the team that last played competitively in the derby almost five years before. A crowd of 32,000 had gathered for the resumption of a football war of attrition and the Blues had struck an early blow by signing Frank Knowles from the Reds just a few days before.

If the people of Manchester had wondered how long it would take for things to get back to normal their concerns were short-lived after perhaps the most thrilling City vs United clash to date – it may have been almost five years in the making, but the 29th derby was well worth the wait.

United were out of the blocks immediately and were ahead within two minutes through James Hodge, but Herbert Taylor brought the Blues level before the break in a breathless first 45 minutes. Joe Spence restored the Reds' lead when he controversially nipped in as City keeper Walter Smith prepared to kick the ball up field, pinching the ball as Smith bounced it on the ground. There was much consternation when the referee awarded the goal, but it made no difference. Angered and determined to right what was felt to be an injustice, Tommy Browell equalized straight from kick-off.

As the game seemingly headed towards a draw United dramatically snatched what seemed a certain winner, through Fred Hopkin's 87th-minute strike. However, while the Reds' contingent was still celebrating, Browell again levelled straight from the restart to earn City a 3-3 draw. The Manchester derby was off and running again and this game had proved what a loss it had been to the people of the city.

Just a week later the teams met again at Old Trafford, with a crowd of 49,000 anticipating another epic, but this time just one goal settled matters, with Joe Spence capitalizing on a rare Eli Fletcher mistake on 71 minutes to give United both points and earn the Reds a first home win for almost a decade – 10 years too long for most Reds' fans! City at least could claim to be top dogs in Manchester again after finishing seventh, while United ended 12th.

United's frustrations would not end there as Ernest Mangnall's City really settled into their stride. The Blues now had players like Max Woosnam among their number – Woosnam was an all-round sports star who could turn his hand to almost anything: he won a gold and silver medal at the 1920 Olympics, scored a century at Lord's, achieved a maximum 147 snooker break and won a doubles title at Wimbledon! The ex-Cambridge Blue was an obvious choice to lead City into a new era and Blues' fans were hoping he would also lead the club into a new period of dominance over United.

He made his debut on 1st January 1920, against Bradford City, a match that also saw the debut of Sam Cookson. Initially, Woosnam played only home matches, due to other commitments. However, when City, without Woosnam, suffered a shock 3-0 FA Cup defeat to Leicester City at the end of the month, some supporters blamed Woosnam's employers, Crossley Brothers. As a result, the engineering firm ordered Woosnam not to miss another game, fearing any other outcome would be bad for business!

Woosnam made his Manchester derby debut on 20th November 1920 in front of a massive 63,000 Old Trafford crowd. Mick Hamill and Wilf Woodcock had continued the trend of players leaving the Reds and joining the Blues, lured by former boss Mangnall, who was clearly well respected by his former charges.

City were now going into derbies as slight favourites. With only a point separating the teams it was always going to be a tight affair, and so it proved with Tommy Miller putting United ahead and Horace Barnes equalizing after the break to complete the scoring.

As had been done the year before the return derby was played just one week later, though circumstances – bizarrely – almost meant another Old Trafford derby.

A fire had destroyed City's Main Stand at Hyde Road, and United offered to ground share as a result. In fact, because the Blues' home could no longer safely house the huge crowds who wanted to attend, United had already offered the more spacious surrounds of Old Trafford previous to the blaze but the Blues declined and instead began sourcing a site for a new stadium of their own.

The fact City now desperately needed a temporary home gave United the edge in any rental negotiations, and when the Reds' board added a clause that any attendance figures in excess of the previous season's corresponding fixture at Hyde Road would be kept by

United, City said thanks, but no thanks. It was a business decision, nothing more, but City still felt they'd been let down. In fact, it was a kick in the teeth for the Blues, who had needed a clause-free offer from United in their time of need.

The Main Stand was hastily replaced by a cinder bank and the capacity increased to 45,000 as a result; the situation made finding a solution all the more pressing. At least a 3-0 win for the Blues eased some of the headaches caused by the fire, even though there were no facilities for washing after the game and the players instead had to change and bathe at a nearby factory.

Max Woosnam was the man of the match as the Blues gave their neighbours something of a thrashing, with goals from Barnes, Browell and Billy "Spud" Murphy all coming in a one-sided first-half. The Blues went on to finish runners-up, just five points behind champions Burnley, while United again finished a disappointing 13th with exactly the same total of 40 points they gathered the previous season.

City looked to kick on for 1921/22 but the decision to re-sign 47-year-old Billy Meredith, who had finally quit Old Trafford after failing to agree a suitable new deal, raised one or two eyebrows.

Meredith had fallen out with United over wage demands and moved back across the city to see out his playing days. It was a bonus for both the player and the City fans, who probably never imagined a reconciliation taking place. He joined as player/coach, but the first true star of British football still had plenty of gas left in his tank and the last thing on his mind was retirement.

With the Reds' glory years now no more than a distant memory, United arrived at Hyde Road in October 1921 fearing the worst, with an ailing side already struggling near the foot of the table, while City looked confident and had their tails up. For once the derby script went as expected and Blues fans revelled in the sight of Meredith tormenting the United defence once again, with Horace Barnes stealing the show in an emphatic 4-1 win. Barnes became the first

City player to score a hat-trick against the Reds, finding the net twice in the first half and completing his treble with a penalty after the break. Joe Spence claimed a consolation goal for the visitors but John Warner completed the rout with a late fourth for the Blues. This was to be the last meeting ever of the Manchester giants at Hyde Road, so this was a fitting epitaph for City's home of 26 years.

Down, but not entirely out, United showed their fighting spirit in the return derby a week later, and 56,000 roared the Reds on to victory. It proved the Blues' neighbours were made of stern stuff too, coming so soon after such a painful defeat.

City had raced into an early lead through Spud Murphy and it looked as though a quick league double would be completed by Mangnall's men, but Joe Spence had other ideas and, just as Barnes had done the week previous, the prolific United forward bagged a hat-trick, scoring twice before half-time and claiming the match ball with a brilliant individual goal 20 minutes from the end. Spence may have stolen the headlines, but the classy display by Meredith had the scribes drooling as he turned back the clock to his heyday with a stunning performance – and to think he'd played in virtually every Manchester derby since 1894 in either a blue or a red shirt! Sadly, this was to be his last appearance in this particular fixture, though he would continue playing for City for another couple of seasons. At least the old man of Manchester football had gone out on a personal high, despite the loss.

The 3-1 win was just the boost the Reds needed, but, with manager John Robson forced to step down due to poor health just two days after the victory, they lost their direction somewhat, failed to capitalize on the feel-good factor and, for the first time in 15 years, United lost their top-flight status by finishing bottom of Division One – a sad demise for one of England's most prominent clubs. City finished 10th but their neighbours' relegation meant they would continue to be top dogs in the city until at least 1925 when the derby would resume once again. By then the Blues had enjoyed 13 years of finishing above United in the league – a fact that caused much consternation in the red half of the city. By the next time the teams met, City would have found a new home…

Blues Make Controversial Move South

1923–1938

"It took just 300 days and £100,000 to construct 'the Wembley of the North' and by 1923 City's new home, Maine Road, was ready to open its doors…"

With United languishing in Division Two, City announced plans for a new stadium, with Hyde Road no longer a viable option for a club of the Blues' standing. Several East Manchester sites were mulled over, with Belle Vue seemingly a natural choice, initially. But, despite the will of many supporters, Belle Vue simply wasn't big enough, with just eight acres available to build on and a lease of just 50 years nowhere near long enough for the grand plans the City board had in mind.

The Blues had watched with envy as Old Trafford was completed, and with a capacity nearly double of Hyde Road the significantly increased crowds gave the Reds greater financial muscle thanks to the bigger gate receipts. City decided their new home would need to blow everything else out of the water and ambitious plans were drawn up for a 120,000-capacity stadium based largely on Scotland's Hampden Park.

A former brickworks in Moss Side seemed perfect for the site of the new stadium and the land was acquired at a cost of £5,500 on a road that used to be called Dog Kennel Lane – though by 1922 it had changed to Maine Road. Renowned architect Charles Swain drew up plans for the huge stadium and, after discussions, it was decided to scale back the capacity to 80,000 – still double the size of Hyde Road.

Some City fans were disappointed at the relocation to South Manchester. One board member even resigned in protest and a few years later formed a new club, Manchester Central, who played their football at Belle Vue, but the project was ill-fated and folded after just a few years.

It took just 300 days and £100,000 to construct "the Wembley of the North" and, by 1923, City's new home, Maine Road, was ready to open its doors. All that was missing for the first couple of years was a Manchester derby, but on 12th September 1925 the battle between the Blues and the Reds resumed and a crowd of 62,994 – easily a new attendance record for City in both the league and for a derby – watched an exciting 1-1 draw. United drew first blood through the grandly-named Clatworthy Rennox, but the Blues' brilliant new centre-half Sam Cowan, playing his first Manchester derby, equalized to earn City, now managed by David Ashworth after Ernest Mangnall decided to call time on his 12-year reign, a point.

That was as good as it got for the Reds who suffered two hammer blows later in the season at the hands of their cross-city rivals.

The return derby at Old Trafford looked, on paper, a home banker. Ashworth's reign had ended in November and the erratic Blues had Albert Alexander Senior – the club's chairman – in charge. The team was capable of brilliance and abject failure, illustrated by an 8-3 home win over Burnley and an 8-3 defeat at Sheffield United just two days later! By the time of the 36th league derby City had seen a total of 129 goals, either scored or conceded, in just 26 games – an average of five goals per game!

United were also capable of winning or losing by considerable margins, so if ever a game was impossible to call this was perhaps the one – and what a match it proved to be, though for a stunned Old Trafford crowd it proved to be something close to torture. Quite simply, City were magnificent on the day, with United unable to stem the constant wave of attacks the visitors fashioned almost from the kick-off. Frank Roberts nodded the Blues ahead from a corner on 18 minutes and Billy Austin, leading the Reds' defence a merry dance, scored a second and then claimed his second assist of the afternoon when Roberts made it 3-0 before the break. With damage limitation in mind United shored their defence for the first 30 minutes after half-time before City's persistence paid off with Tommy Johnson, Austin and George Hicks putting the visitors 6-0 up. It was incredible stuff and Rennox's late consolation almost added insult to injury for the shell-shocked United fans, who knew they would need to keep their heads low for a few weeks at least.

The one thing about a Manchester derby drubbing is that there is nowhere to hide for the losers! And there was more pain to come for the Reds and their supporters when the two teams met again in the FA Cup semi-final clash at Bramall Lane just eight weeks later. Tommy Browell (2) and Frank Roberts ensured a 3-0 win for the Blues who went on to lose the final to Bolton Wanderers at Wembley.

Yet, despite the highs against United and the fact 89 goals had been scored in the league, City were relegated after finishing in 21st place in the table.

The Blues would take two years to return to the top flight, finishing third in their first attempt – this after missing out by an unbelievable five thousandths of a goal to Portsmouth in the closest goal average finish in league history – and then winning Division Two at a canter (scoring 100 goals or more on each occasion).

Maine Road had been in service for five years but was still yet to taste a derby victory when the teams met on 1st September 1928. Another huge crowd of 61,007 had gathered, and with recent results in mind this fixture was almost torturous for both sets of fans, with the fear of defeat all-consuming in the run-up to the game. With changes to the offside law now in operation and favouring attackers more, United would ultimately blow their chance of a first Maine Road victory after confusion in their defence led to City earning a 2-2 draw. Roberts had given City the lead but United roared back with Jack Wilson and Billy Johnston sending the Reds in 2-1 up at the break. But with only two opponents now needed between the striker and the goal line instead of three, clever strikers were finding more opportunities than ever before, and a misjudgement by United defender Jack Silcock allowed Tommy Johnson to streak through almost unchallenged to score the goal that earned City a share of the spoils.

When, wondered City fans, would their team ever beat the Reds in Moss Side?

Meanwhile, United fans had waited almost three painful years to banish the memory of the 6-1 defeat in the last meeting at Old Trafford, so when Bill Rawlings put the Reds ahead in the 38th league derby the majority of the 42,555 began to relax a little thinking it was payback time. Neither side were setting the division on fire and were casting anxious glances over their shoulders as the spectre of relegation refused to go away. City were keen to avoid a quick return to the second tier and equalized immediately through Billy Austin, chief tormentor during the 6-1 thrashing, and City stole both points when Tommy Johnson scored a late winner to make it 2-1. Both Manchester clubs ended the season in mid-table; City's victory in the derby saw them finish eighth with the Reds in 12th.

Ten months later, City recorded a third successive Old Trafford win and United fans wondered when they could again actually enjoy this fixture. Tommy Johnson, Bobby Marshall and Eric Brook were all on the mark, with Henry Thomas replying for the hosts. A 3-1 win was sweet enough, but as Johnson rolled the ball home for number four after rounding United keeper Lewis Barber on 88 minutes to complete a brilliant goal, the referee blew for full-time – more than two minutes early! The official also claimed he'd blown as the ball reached the goal line but every watch in the house showed only 87 and a half minutes had passed. It was suspicious to say the least and denied City yet another demolition derby victory, though the victory was welcomed all the same.

With Maine Road crowds now dwarfing those at Old Trafford by up to 20,000, the latest gate of 64,472 suggested the power shift in the city had firmly swung in the direction of City – yet that elusive first derby victory in Moss Side would still not come. With the Blues' new home now seven years old United continued their proud unbeaten run at Maine Road with a victory to go with their previous two draws. It was a title blow to Peter Hodge's loftily-placed side who were patchy at best and never reached anywhere near the standard of the Old Trafford victory four months prior. Tom Reid's 15th-minute goal was enough to ease United's relegation fears and restore pride, though they would finish 14 places lower than City in 17th position. Clearly, there was work to be done on both sides of the city if silverware was once again going to make its way back to Manchester though, for the Reds, the urgency was far greater.

Mancunian football was about to hit a new low with the 41st derby seeing City go into the game with just one win in their opening eight games, United having lost all of theirs. In fact, so bad were the Reds, gates had slipped as low as 11,000 and there were supporters' protests and boycotts as their supporters wondered just how their club had been allowed to fall from grace so dramatically. For an equally lacklustre City team this was manna from heaven and the Blues mercilessly set about making United's plight twice as bad with a thumping 4-1 win at Maine Road – the Blues' first win over the old enemy at their new home. A brace each for Bobby Marshall and Tommy Tait delighted most of the 47,757 crowd. With the Reds reduced to eight men, through a series of injuries, and City down to nine, as the game wore the match took on farcical proportions. Joe Spence's sixth Manchester derby goal was the only consolation for a United side in total disarray both on and off the pitch.

With the Depression hitting Britain hard United were intertwined in a depression of their own making, and with the vast crowds of a decade ago long gone and the club just managing to keep its head above water financially, City once again arrived looking to compound their neighbours' misery.

Promising young Scot Matt Busby made his one and only derby appearance for the Blues in this game and United battled well, with Spence equalizing Eric Brook's thunderbolt shot earlier in the game. With 87 goals conceded by United there was an inevitability that the Blues would, at some point, score again and probably take both points, and with 10 minutes left the Reds' resistance finally ended as Brook laid on a perfect cross for Ernie Toseland to make it 2-1, and then he set up a decisive third for David Halliday to make it 3-1 moments later. It was City's fourth successive win at Old Trafford and, with just two defeats in 11 trips to the Reds' home, this was a game City fans were eagerly looking forward to each season. Of course there would be a wait for the next opportunity to build on that impressive run as the Reds were relegated after the end of the most miserable season in the club's history. It wouldn't get better in a hurry, either. United had to be saved from bankruptcy by local businessman James Gibson and spent five years in the wilderness of Division Two, while City established themselves as a fantastic FA Cup team reaching the semi-final in 1932 then the final in 1933 (losing to Everton) before recording a second triumph in the competition a year later with a 2-1 win over Portsmouth. In 1934 only a final day victory over Millwall spared United the ignominy of dropping into Division Three, but the green shoots of recovery began thereafter and by the end of the 1935/36 campaign – after a five year absence – the Reds returned to the top flight. Division One and Manchester needed a good United side, but there was still a lot of hard work ahead.

If envious glances were cast across the city by United it was understandable. The Blues had assembled a stellar side that included keeper Frank Swift and gifted inside-forward Peter Doherty. Maine Road had set a new attendance record outside Wembley, with almost 85,000 watching the Blues beat Stoke City 1-0 in 1934, and crowds regularly topping 60,000.

Many felt if City were ever going to win the Division One title it would be now, but United dealt Wilf Wild's men an early blow with a 3-2 win at Old Trafford to bring further cheer to the United faithful who were once again starting to believe in their team. Tommy Bamford and Tommy Manley put the Reds 2-0 up as City struggled in the mud to find their normal passing game. But this City side was made of stern stuff and Jackie Bray and Jimmy Heale brought the Blues back to level terms. In an entertaining encounter nobody would have complained if the match had finished 2-2, but United had one last ace up their sleeve in the form of winger William Bryant who won the game for the hosts on 81 minutes to send Old Trafford wild.

The teams resumed battle in January and only six points separated the Manchester rivals. Alec Herd scored the only goal for City in a 1-0 win, and the Blues would go on and remain unbeaten for the rest of the season – a run of 20 league matches without defeat – and lift their first ever top-flight title. The championship was achieved in style, too, with 107 goals scored and some fantastic football played. For United fans it was almost too much to bear as they saw their team meekly slip out of Division One after just one season. For Manchester football such a gaping chasm was not good, and with the Second World War on the horizon these two proud clubs would not meet in the league again for a decade; however, there was to be one final twist before the nation once again went to war...

Champs to Chumps and the Red Revival

1938–1953

"There's no war in this dressing room. We welcome you as we would any other member of staff."

City skipper Eric Westwood, 1949

Imagine the odds: the defending league champions are not only to lose their crown but face losing their top-flight status too.

In a remarkable change of fortune United won promotion the same season City were relegated, meaning that it would be the Reds rather than the Blues who could justifiably claim the bragging rights for the next few years. The 1938/39 campaign was the last before the war, and with no derby and neither side relegated or promoted, Mancunians, like the rest of the country, would have to wait until 1945 before league action resumed. Three games were played of the 1939/40 season, but league football was then suspended as the seriousness of the conflict with Germany put the importance of football into context.

What followed over the next six years was a series of regional leagues and cup competitions, with both teams made up of contracted players, amateurs and guests. The crowds were poor – often no more than 5,000 – and in truth the games were more for morale than entertainment. People needed some semblance of normality and if City and United, as well as other league clubs around the country, were still playing it helped keep spirits up during an

37

incredibly difficult period for millions of people.

There were numerous Manchester derbies but they were pale imitations of the real thing and so frequent that they were viewed as little more than meaningless friendlies. Then, on 11th March 1945, a German Luftwaffe air attack scored a direct hit on Old Trafford, reducing much of United's home to rubble, with the main stand destroyed and the pitch badly damaged. As if the war wasn't bad enough, now there would be a daily reminder of the conflict on one of the few patches of green left in the city. United fans wondered if life could get any worse.

Fortunately, there was help at hand as City immediately offered to share Maine Road until Old Trafford was repaired; with rationing and a lack of skilled workers and material to reconstruct the Reds' home, the ground share arrangement would last for eight years. While hostilities raged across Europe the Manchester clubs proved that, no matter what, each would look after the other in times of great need.

More than 150 players represented City during the war, and league action finally resumed in 1946 following the Allies' victory over Adolf Hitler's Nazi Germany.

United had, by that time, employed former City star Matt Busby as their manager. The Reds had tried to buy Busby when he was a City player, but had been turned down. Busby had been involved with Liverpool, but United were offering the manager's job, and a friend of Busby's, who was well-connected at United, promised the Reds' board he would deliver Busby as the new boss. After writing to him in the Army – but not stating the exact reason why he was being invited to Old Trafford – Busby arrived to listen to what the United hierarchy had to say. He was interested in becoming the manager provided it was on his terms. That included final say on the coaching, style and transfers – unprecedented power at that time – but he got his way and was offered a three-year deal, which he argued up to five years on account of how long he felt his project would take to see fruition.

It was a shrewd piece of business by Busby, but it laid foundations for a dynasty that would forever change the fortunes of Manchester United FC.

Meanwhile the Blues, initially, stuck with long-serving boss Wilf Wild; but a few months into the 1946/47 season one of City's favourite sons, Sam Cowan, was appointed manager and the former skipper guided City to the Division Two title in his first season in charge. With the nation still in celebratory mood, Manchester, too, could celebrate the fact it once again had both of its teams back in the top division.

The derbies of the late 1940s would have one notable difference to those before the war; however, with both games being played at Maine Road, and for the first derby in a decade, it was fitting that City's home fixture against the Reds should attract the biggest crowd ever for a meeting between the two clubs – 78,000 – as the people of the city welcomed back its showpiece sporting fixture. In a bizarre twist, however, the Blues would have to take on the Reds without manager Cowan who was forced to resign after refusing to relocate north. Cowan had a successful physiotherapy practice near Brighton and enjoyed life on the south coast. He felt he could continue to commute and do both roles successfully but club officials were concerned his 260-mile trips to Manchester were detrimental to the club and playing staff, so despite guiding the Blues to promotion at the first attempt, his resignation was (presumably) reluctantly accepted. John Thomson took over from Cowan.

With so much anticipation ahead of the 45th Manchester derby it was maybe predictable that the game failed to live up to expectations and, after a frustrating 90 minutes, neither side managed to find a way through the other's defence and the match ended 0-0.

Matt Busby, meanwhile, was astutely building a strong team who played attractive football and he was already proving to be a bright young manager. He had taken the role on aged just 35 –

almost unheard of at that time – and was moulding United into a side with real quality. The return derby saw the Reds very much in the ascendancy but the fact their "home" derby was again at Maine Road meant there was little or no territorial advantage for United, but they were certainly winning new fans; many believed some "floating" City fans may have done the unthinkable and switched allegiance around this time. The Blues had been top dogs in terms of success and crowds for the majority of the past 25 years but it was United who averaged almost 55,000 while City averaged just shy of 42,000.

With 71,690 watching the latest derby a 1-1 draw was a more than respectable result for City, who had led through a Billy Linacre goal before Jack Rowley levelled for the Reds.

United went on to lift the FA Cup shortly after with a thrilling 4-2 win over Blackpool at Wembley where the Reds turned a 2-1 deficit into victory with three goals in the last 20 minutes, and also finished runners-up to Arsenal in Division One, whereas City settled for consolidation and a 10th-placed finish.

The 1948/49 season again saw both derbies played at Maine Road though, with restoration work to Old Trafford well under way, it would be the last season at least one of the teams would call Moss Side their home. Each meeting ended 0-0 meaning the last four derbies had produced just two goals and four successive stalemates but, more worryingly for City, it had been 13 years since they'd last tasted victory.

The 1949/50 season wouldn't improve matters either with the Reds back home at Old Trafford and winning both derbies by a 2-1 margin. The first meeting saw City ahead on 34 minutes, when Jimmy Munro scored with a long-range effort, and for 75 minutes it seemed as though that might be enough to win the game and end the Blues' winless streak. But Stan Pearson had other ideas and after levelling via a hotly disputed goalmouth melee he then hit a sweetly struck winner shortly after. United's Henry Cockburn and Billy Linacre were both sent off in the dying moments as tempers boiled over, but Matt Busby's men hung on for the win.

The Maine Road derby – the 50th league meeting between the clubs – was the Blues' former German prisoner of war goalkeeper Bert Trautmann's first taste of local rivalry. The protestations of Trautmann's signing were long and loud with City receiving hundreds of letters demanding the former Nazi be kicked out of the club. Trautmann had exercised his right to remain in England after being captured during the conflict and, after meeting a local girl, he began playing for St Helen's Town, where word quickly got around that he was a goalie of some talent. The Blues decided Trautmann was worth the trouble his signing would cause, and over the course of the next 15 years or so it would prove to be an inspired move.

Trautmann's derby bow was astonishingly similar to the last meeting in that City struck first – Andy Black was on target this time – only for United to hit back with two goals to win 2-1. Jimmy Delaney equalized, and, again, Stan Pearson was on hand to score a dramatic late winner. In each game City had gone close to going 2-0 up, hitting the bar at Old Trafford and having a goal controversially rubbed out at Maine Road – had the Blues' luck been different and a goal been scored on each occasion, they would have ended with four more points and finished one place higher than United. Instead they were relegated and once more had to navigate their way out of the second tier as quickly as possible.

United finished fourth, just three points adrift of champions Portsmouth after another enjoyable season under Busby. In fact, United finished runners-up for the 1950/51 campaign – the fourth time in five years they'd narrowly missed out on the title – and City also finished runners-up in Division Two to quickly restore their top-flight status. Supporting either Manchester club was, at times, a breathless experience and there never seemed to be a dull moment in the city.

Where derby matters were concerned, however, little changed for the Blues as they slumped to a third successive 2-1 defeat to United at Maine Road. Johnny Berry put the visitors ahead after just nine minutes but City fought back and levelled on 54 minutes through Johnny Hart; however, just as had happened in the previous two losses the Reds stole a late winner through Harry McShane to leave City fans almost dreading derby day, so often did it end in misery. Had it really been 14 years since they'd last enjoyed a victory?

The Old Trafford return saw City take the lead yet again only to fail to go and win yet again – it was the sixth time in nine derbies the Blues had scored first but somehow squandered their advantage. Still, Frank McCourt's spectacular effort wasn't entirely in vain as United could only manage a draw on this occasion, courtesy of Johnny Carey's low drive. The consistent Reds went on to win their second title four months later finishing four points clear of second placed Tottenham Hotspur. City, now under the tutelage of Les McDowall, had to settle for 15th.

The Blues' long wait for a derby victory finally ended in August 1952 when goals from Roy Clarke and Ivor Broadis established a 2-0 lead that United, on this occasion, could not recover from, though they did pull a late goal back through John Downie to ensure a tense finish. It was a particularly sweet win for the 56,140 City fans who had endured 15 years of hurt and disappointment – and the fact United were the defending champions gave the victory even more resonance.

Bragging rights stayed with the Blue half of Manchester after City earned a creditable 1-1 draw at Old Trafford. Long-time thorn in City's side, Stan Pearson, struck a fierce shot past Trautmann, but the Blues levelled on the hour thanks to Ivor Broadis. It proved a vital point, too, with City finishing in 20th position, just one point ahead of relegated Stoke City. The Reds surrendered their Division

One crown with a disappointing eighth-placed finish. The next few seasons, however, would see a boom time for Manchester football...

The Busby Babes and City Roar Back

1953–1957

"In all modesty, my summing up of 1955–56 and 1956–57 must be that no club in the country could live with Manchester United."

Matt Busby

It is rare that both Manchester clubs are in the ascendency – moreover, the Reds and Blues had, thus far, seemed to take turns in being top dogs, with one set of fans usually on a high and lording over their neighbours and the other group unable to hold their heads high.

United had enjoyed the better of the post-war years and that would continue into the 1953/54 season, though it would be relegation threatened City who would enjoy the bragging rights for this campaign.

Neither side made an impressive start to the season and were both rooted close to the foot of Division One. Ivor Broadis, one of City's stellar talents, had been surprisingly transfer listed following a fall-out with manager Les McDowall; there was a general feeling of discontent at Maine Road, with recent developments suggesting the Blues were still a long way from challenging again for major honours.

City's team contained some great names including Trautmann, Don Revie and Roy Paul, while United had strengthened with Dennis Viollet and Tommy Taylor bolstering Matt Busby's squad; yet none of the Reds' big names really turned up on the day, with one newspaper suggesting the United attack was "the worst for 20 years".

Second-half goals from Johnny Hart and Revie gave City a 2-0 win and ensured United dropped to their lowest league position yet under Busby. However, by the return at Old Trafford four months later, United had steadily moved up the table and were eight points clear of the Blues – and that looked set to increase to 10 thanks to Johnny Berry's first-half goal. Only Trautmann's brilliance was keeping City in the game and, though time had seemingly ran out and the referee had checked his watch at least once, Roy Clarke jinked past Bill Foulkes before passing to Billy McAdams who struck firmly past Ray Wood to earn the Blues a 1-1 draw.

United finished in fourth that season while City languished near the trap door yet again, finishing 17th – though things were about to improve – and how!

Les McDowall decided on a tactical switch within his teams that instantly began to pay dividends. Having watched the brilliant Hungary side end England's unbeaten record at Wembley with a stunning 5-1 win McDowall decided to adopt a similar formation at City, pulling striker Don Revie away from the traditional centre-forward role and instead giving him something of a license to roam just in front of the midfield. It was simple yet revolutionary and confused opposition defences who weren't sure how to deal with Revie or City's wide men. United would, in particular, find the new system difficult to deal with. By the time of the 57th derby "the Revie Plan" had helped the Blues challenge near the top; just two points separated the Manchester clubs.

It was to be a thrilling derby – one of the best in years – and City raced out of the blocks with Revie, a pivotal figure, eluding the United back four and creating space for others to the point United simply didn't know how to handle him. Billy McAdams and Paddy Fagan deservedly put the Blues 2-0 up within 20 minutes before Taylor finally gave United a foothold in the game. City were not to be denied, and clever movement from Revie created a chance for Hart that the City forward tucked away with aplomb. United weren't finished yet, though, and Jackie Blanchflower made it 3-2 to set up a nail-biting finish that saw the Reds twice hit the woodwork before the final whistle ended the contest that, in truth, either side would have been worthy winners of.

United were again out-foxed by the Blues at Maine Road during a fourth-round FA Cup match. Revie and Joe Hayes were both on the mark in the 2-0 win and there was more misery to come for the Reds' young team, dubbed "the Busby Babes". It was perhaps the inexperience that was baffling United and, just two weeks after the FA Cup exit, Busby's side suffered a chastening defeat to City for the third time that season.

Revie again pulled the strings to great effect and, after a superb passing move, pulled United apart and ended with Hart beating Wood from Hayes' cross. That would be the only goal of the first half, with the Reds rallying for the remainder of the opening 45 but unable to beat Trautmann. United again came at City after the restart but, with Revie almost unplayable, Fagan and Hayes profited from the No.9's brilliance to put the contest out of United's reach – though there was more punishment to come as the same players each scored another goal to give City an emphatic 5-0 win in their neighbours' backyard. The margin of victory matched the 6-1 win back in 1926 and left the Blues fans purring through the summer months despite finishing two places lower than fifth-placed United. The only downside to a fine season for McDowall's team was the 3-1 FA Cup final defeat to Newcastle United two months after the Old Trafford romp. City fans now craved silverware to go with their exciting team and they wouldn't have to wait much longer.

The 1955/56 campaign proved to be a stellar year for Manchester football with both of English football's major domestic honours making their way back to the city. The Busby Babes came of age in the league and would go on to win Division One with style and panache, while City made a triumphant return to Wembley to lift the FA Cup.

The Blues would take the honours in the first meeting at Maine Road thanks, in part, to Joe Hayes' solitary strike, but mostly due to the brilliant display of Trautmann in the City goal; United gained revenge in the Old Trafford return. Jack Dyson, an accomplished first-class cricketer with Lancashire, made his derby debut a day to remember by putting the Blues ahead in front of almost 61,000 fans – with 20,000 more locked out. City knew if they could end United's unbeaten home record they would also severely dent the league leaders' title hopes. But the Busby Babes hadn't climbed to the top of the pile by luck and, when the visitors' defence misjudged a strong gust of wind, Tommy Taylor nipped in to equalize and send Old Trafford wild. Then Dennis Viollet put the Reds ahead from a corner to put United 2-1 up. There was still time for Roy Clarke to hit the bar, but the Reds clung on for the victory – their first in 10 attempts – and continued on their way to their third league title, with the Blues finishing a very respectable fourth. With City beating Birmingham 3-1 in the FA Cup final – "the Trautmann final" after City's brave German custodian broke his neck making a save and then incredibly continued playing for the final 15 minutes – the 1955/56 season proved to be Manchester's finest yet. The Blues' goalkeeper also won the respect of the nation for his bravery and courage at Wembley, especially when examinations revealed one more knock could have left him paralysed.

With United in rampant form the Busby Babes would win all three of the derby meetings in 1956/57. Goals from Viollet and Billy Whelan gave the Reds a 2-0 league win at Old Trafford in September, and then Viollet again struck the winner in the FA Charity Shield meeting at Maine Road in October watched by a crowd of just over 30,000. It was the first meeting between the Manchester clubs in what was usually the annual curtain raiser, but the original date had proved unsuitable so the autumnal clash perhaps carried less interest to the paying fan. The match, originally planned for Old Trafford but switched due to floodlight issues, was nevertheless played with a competitive edge and was in many ways a tale of two keepers. The Blues were still without Trautmann, who was recovering from his broken neck injury, and John Savage deputized in his absence. Meanwhile, United's No.1 Ray Wood lasted just 40 minutes of the contest before retiring with injury. With substitutes now in operation the Reds were forced to bring on sub keeper David Gaskell – nothing unusual there – except he was still only 15! Despite his tender years and lack of experience Gaskell went on to have a largely untroubled game, with City failing to put him under any real pressure, and he would end the game with a debut clean sheet and a winners' medal, as United team-mate Dennis Viollet's 75th-minute goal settled a disappointing contest.

There was worse to come for City, too – but ecstasy for Reds' fans – as United returned three months later to complete their biggest Maine Road victory to date. Don Revie had been sold to Sunderland and, with his departure, so ended the Revie Plan that had caused United so many problems in recent years. At least Trautmann had returned to full fitness, but the Reds were on a roll and City were struggling near the foot of the table when the teams met at Maine Road in February 1957.

Jack Dyson should have put City ahead in the early exchanges, but Billy Whelan scored not long after, following an uncharacteristic slip by Bill Leivers; Blues followers had a feeling this wasn't going to be their day. Roy Clarke managed to level the scores but United stormed back, through Tommy Taylor and Dennis Viollet, to establish a 3-1 lead and delight the travelling fans in the 63,872 crowd. Duncan Edwards then extinguished any lingering hopes City would fight back before Joe Hayes scored a late consolation to make it

2-4 in United's favour. It was the first time in more than 20 years that the Reds had scored more than two goals in a derby – home or away – and also the first time they managed more than two goals at Maine Road. The celebrations lasted well into the night in the red strongholds of the city.

While the Blues' recent progress ended with a very disappointing 18th-place finish, United were again top dogs in the city – and England – with a second successive league title. City had plenty of catching up to do...

Munich and the Rebirth of the Reds

1957–1962

> "*Even City fans, however, would not deny Gregg deserved to take something from the game. The Reds' keeper had become a hero to thousands of youngsters fascinated by his bravery as a man and his ability as a goalkeeper.*"

No one could have predicted the dramatic events of the 1957/58 season or the tragedy and loss of human life that Manchester United would suffer as they returned from a European Cup tie against Red Star Belgrade. City, too, would lose one of their most cherished sons in an accident that changed so much for both clubs. For United, many wondered how the club could ever recover from what was to be such a devastating loss.

The campaign began as the previous one had ended with United, the defending champions, enjoying the better of the derby spoils.

The Reds had raced out of the blocks with two emphatic victories over Leicester and Everton, while City had seen off Chelsea at Stamford Bridge. There was real hope that the Blues would challenge the Reds' recent dominance, but the first derby of the season on 31st August suggested it may take a little longer. City were lambs to the slaughter at Old Trafford, losing 4-1. Goals from Berry, Edwards, Viollet and Taylor were answered only by Ken Barnes' solitary strike in front of 63,103 Old Trafford fans. By the time the teams reconvened at Maine Road, however, free-scoring City were hot on the heels of their neighbours who were just one place above them in the table in fourth. The match, too, would be a far more even battle ending 2-2 after a hugely entertaining 90 minutes. Hayes and a Bill Foulkes own goal accounted for City's goals, while Viollet scored for the sixth derby in succession, and a very young Bobby Charlton found the net in his first ever game against City.

By February United were in third and six points adrift of leaders Wolves, with City trailing the Reds by three points. Then, on 6th February 1958, as United returned from Belgrade via a fuel stop in Munich, their British European Airways plane crashed on take-off. The flight should have been cancelled until better conditions prevailed, but the pilot felt there was no reason why his plane shouldn't successfully take off. After two dramatic aborted attempts to take off, the third and final attempt saw the aircraft again fail to get airborne but, critically, pass the speed needed to safely abort and instead continue to hurtle down the runway. Slush would later be identified as a major cause of the crash that resulted when the plane smashed into a building at the end of the runway. Of the 44 passengers on board 23 would die, including eight Manchester United players. Geoff Bent, Roger Byrne, Eddie Colman, Duncan Edwards, Mark Jones, David Pegg, Tommy Taylor and Billy Whelan all lost their lives – Edwards initially survived but died later in hospital as a result of his injuries – and former City great Frank Swift, working as a journalist covering United's game for the *News of the World*, also perished in the crash. The condition of manager Matt Busby was so bad he received the Last Rites on two occasions; but his will was strong, and with the prayers of the football world to carry him on he somehow pulled through. After nine weeks he was finally discharged from hospital. It had been nothing short of a miracle that he had pulled through. Clearly, there was a job for Matt Busby still to finish, and he would recover to steer United to their greatest triumphs in future years. For now, however, there was only disbelief. The city of Manchester was in shock, as was the rest of the nation, Europe and the world. All rivalry was set aside and grief and sympathy took its place. Manchester truly was a city united in every sense.

Life and football, however, went on, as it had to. United somehow completed their fixtures, reaching the FA Cup final where they lost 2-0 to Bolton Wanderers (the team included four survivors from Munich), and the European Cup semi-final. They had been carried on a wave of emotion but had finally run out of steam, physically and mentally drained, in the final weeks of the season. That City finished fourth and United ninth mattered little; football seemed unimportant. The fact City had become the first club to score and concede 100 goals in a season was forgotten, though in later years it would become a favourite trivia question and, quite rightly, was regarded as quite a feat in its own right.

The first derby after the Munich disaster was on 27th September 1958 and was understandably a muted, emotional affair. United had begun to rebuild their squad, signing Albert Quixall for a British transfer record of £45,000 from Sheffield Wednesday, but it was one of the plane crash survivors who gave the Reds a third-minute lead. Bobby Charlton was fouled in the box and stepped up to successfully convert the spot-kick to give his side the advantage but City were also awarded a first-half penalty. Ken Barnes saw his attempt well saved by Harry Gregg – the hero of the air crash for his selfless acts of bravery in rescuing others from the plane wreck.

The Blues did draw level just before half-time when Joe Hayes finally found a way past Gregg to make it 1-1. While a point was satisfactory all round City fans left Maine Road still talking about one moment of controversy that overshadowed all else: Ray Sambrook seemed to have put City 2-1 up, and as the fans celebrated and the ball was returned to the centre spot, a persistent linesman finally caught the referee's attention and the goal was disallowed – with no obvious explanation.

Even City fans, however, would not deny Gregg deserved to take something from the game. The Reds' keeper had become a hero to thousands of youngsters fascinated by his bravery as a man and his ability as a goalkeeper.

United, maybe driven on by emotion as well as talent, were challenging strongly for the title again, while the Blues, clearly in decline, were struggling to stay in the division by the time the teams met at Old Trafford. The Reds had won nine of their previous 10 league games, City had won just two of their last 10 – it showed, too, as United romped home 4-1 a year and eight days on from the first anniversary of the disaster at Munich. It was a remarkable achievement and goals from Freddie Goodwin, Warren Bradley (2) and Albert Scanlon meant Bobby Johnstone's solitary effort was in vain. The Reds were clearly back, and finishing runners-up to Wolves was testament to the character of the players and their manager, Matt Busby.

Neither Manchester club tore up trees in the 1959/60 campaign. United could at least claim to have clocked up a century of goals as they finished seventh, while City improved marginally, finishing in 16th, three points above relegated Nottingham Forest.

Going into the derby that season City were at their unpredictable worst and, while they were capable of losing heavily, they could also turn on the style on occasion making them both fascinating and infuriating in equal measure. Positioned in 17th with United in eighth, and also having some odd results, winning 6-0 one week, losing 5-1 the next, this match was impossible to call!

Despite the gloom surrounding the Blues, as it transpired, it was they who claimed the bragging rights for the first time in a few years after two Joe Hayes goals – his eighth and ninth in this fixture making him the club's all-time leading scorer in derby games – and another from George Hannah gave Les McDowall's side a 3-0 Maine Road victory in September, again proving that they weren't far away from being a decent side if they could lose their inconsistency. The teams met at Old Trafford on the second anniversary of Munich to share the points in a 0-0 draw. It didn't happen often but United's derby crowd was larger than City's by a few hundred. The Manchester crowds would level off for a few years before gradually United's became larger. City were in the middle of a barren period with little prospect of improvement and a lack of funds to drastically turn their fortunes around.

The Blues' painful decline reached a new low during the 1960/61 season with two soul-destroying defeats to United.

The first proved to be a record low with even the brilliant Trautmann unable to prevent City going down to their worst Old Trafford defeat. Seven defeats in their previous eight games suggested Les McDowall's era was coming to an end and, in modern times, this derby drubbing may well have been the end of the Blues' long-serving manager. Several new signings had been made but it was the young Scot from Huddersfield Town, Denis Law, who caught the eye in the early weeks of the campaign for City.

United were ahead early on through Bobby Charlton but Colin Barlow levelled the scores shortly after. Alex Dawson made it 2-1 to the Reds after 20 minutes before the Blues dug in and attempted to find a foot-hold in the game. The truth was there wasn't enough quality in the side to do that, and Dawson and Charlton helped themselves to another goal each shortly after the break in quick succession. Dawson completed his hat-trick near the end to make it 5-1 for the Reds.

The Maine Road derby on New Year's Eve 1960 suggested a dark decade ahead for City and the next meeting seemed to back this up. Dawson again was on the mark as wind and rain swept across Moss Side, but City were furious after the United man appeared to put the ball in the net with his hand. Barrie Betts then missed a penalty for City and watched in agony as Charlton spectacularly doubled United's lead not long after. Dave Wagstaffe pulled one back, but Mark Pearson settled matters with a third that left the Blues just three points off the bottom and looking like relegation certainties. City rallied in the final stretch, and three wins and four draws in the last seven games ensured McDowall's men survived fairly comfortably in the end.

United continued to dominate the fixture over the next two seasons with the first meeting of the 1961/62 campaign at Old Trafford easily the most entertaining. With the Reds going into the game in second and City having rallied just behind in third, this game was worthy of its top-of-the-table billing. Nobby Stiles put United ahead in the blink of an eye and Dennis Viollet made it 2-0 with only 14 minutes on the clock. City fans feared another hammering, similar to the 5-1 defeat they'd suffered nine months earlier, but Stiles' name went into the history books when he sliced a clearance past Harry Gregg and into his own net before the break – becoming the first player to score at both ends in a derby match – and then Bobby Kennedy sent the City fans wild when he unleashed a 30-yard pile-driver to make it 2-2. It was thrilling stuff and epitomized everything that was good about the Manchester derby.

There was to be one more decisive own goal, however, as Dave Ewing's attempt to clear a Viollet shot resulted in his diverting the ball past Trautmann for what proved to be the winner for the hosts. The result seemed to dent City's confidence irreparably and the Blues embarked on a terrible run that eventually saw them go from being top in September to bottom in December. United failed to win any of their next nine games and Manchester had the ignominy of seeing both its clubs go from second and third top to second and third bottom in the same period of time. It was unthinkable that both could face relegation, but both clubs staged a decent second half of the season to finish in mid-table, though United's 2-0 win at Maine Road in February wasn't enough to see them finish above the Blues, who were three places higher than Matt Busby's men in 12th. It was impossible to predict what would happen next in the theatre that was Manchester football.

Separate Ways

1962–1967

"Both teams continued to underwhelm their fans and, by the time the teams met at Maine Road, each knew a victory would likely be enough to avoid the drop while sending the other down."

The writing had been on the wall for some time and the 1962/63 season would see Manchester lose one of its giants to relegation in a dismal campaign for both United and City.

Defensively the Blues were a shambles. Trautmann, though still capable of brilliance, was in his 13th season for City and was coming to the end of a glittering career, and this would be Les McDowall's 12th and final season as manager at Maine Road. United weren't much better with the remnants of the Busby Babes mixed with, frankly, several inferior signings who weren't up to the task.

The Reds, at least, had a new idol to worship following the purchase of former City striker Denis Law from Torino. Law had spent one memorable season in sky blue before leaving to join the Italian side for a record £100,000 – money too good for City to refuse – but now he was back and playing in red. Law was meant to play for the Reds, and in his new surrounds he soon acclaimed the royal throne that would lead United fans to simply call him "the King" as time went on.

The Blues couldn't have had a worse start to the campaign, with a woeful 8-1 opening day defeat to a rampant Wolves side. United made an equally disappointing start and, by the time the teams met at Old Trafford in mid-September, it appeared both were trying to out-do the other in the battle for bottom spot.

In front of less than 50,000, City found themselves up against former golden boy Law for the first time. He showed why he was such a coveted talent by scoring twice for the Reds on the day, but Peter Dobing, veteran Joe Hayes and Alex Harley secured a 3-2 win, and only a second victory over the Reds in 15 attempts.

Both teams continued to underwhelm their fans and, by the time the teams met at Maine Road, each knew a victory would likely be enough to avoid the drop while sending the other down. Two points for City would leave United still masters of their own destiny with one game in hand but with huge pressure on them going into their final two games. City thought they'd done enough, going ahead through Alex Harley after just nine minutes to delight the majority of the near-60,000 crowd. Harley then seemed to have made it 2-0, but the "goal" was disallowed, infuriating the City players.

Then, with nails bitten, players squaring up to one another and the tension almost unbearable, the game entered its final five minutes and, as Wagstaffe opted for safety instead of clearing the ball away, his back pass was read by Law, who collided with keeper Harry Dowd, before seeing the ball harmlessly trickle wide. To the dismay of the Blues, however, the referee decided the challenge was illegal and pointed to the spot. Albert Quixall kept his head to make it 1-1 and earn a point for the Reds, leaving Maine Road shell-shocked.

City went into their final game needing a win and needing Birmingham to lose, but the Blues crumbled 6-1 at West Ham. Birmingham won their game at a previously unbeaten-at-home Leicester City, and so the Blues were relegated. The Reds had done just enough and survived by three points, but they would rub their neighbours' noses in the mud by then winning the FA Cup against Leicester a week later.

George Poyser was appointed the Blues' new boss but, as City struggled to come to terms with life in the second tier, the Reds had regenerated themselves and finished runners-up in the league in 1963/64, and then won the title the season after – their sixth to date.

Poyser was in charge for two unsuccessful seasons before being moved on and replaced by a new-look managerial team of Joe Mercer and Malcolm Allison.

Mercer had been forced out of Aston Villa after suffering ill health but he felt he could continue in management, given enough rest.

At Villa he had taken on too much – in addition to the playing side he was also a major player in the development of a new stand – and while he lay at home ill, the Villa board decided to terminate his contract. Villa's loss was City's gain.

After a year out of the game he joined the Blues. His doctor had tried to dissuade him but admitted to Mercer's wife, Norah: "He may as well die doing the job he loves, than sit at home and die of a broken heart."

Mercer was determined to prove his former employers wrong. He said: "The chance was irresistible. I knew that people had written me off. There were doubts about my health, but I had no lack of confidence about my ability. Malcolm Allison was magnificent and I knew he would make the perfect right-hand man. I knew we had a chance with Manchester City. Although they were in the Second Division they were a club with a tradition and a ready-made public."

In Mercer and Allison's debut season the green shoots of recovery began in earnest with promotion and the Division Two title secured during the 1965/66 campaign.

It was just the fillip the blue half of the city needed and, for Manchester football, it meant the resumption of the derby after an absence of more than three years.

Having already brought Mike Summerbee to Maine Road from Swindon, Mercer added 30-year-old Tony Book from Plymouth and

Colin Bell from Bury.

Book, a former bricklayer, was well known to Allison who had coached him at Bath City and Plymouth, and he would become the Blues' new captain. Bell, signed for £50,000 from Bury, was one of the country's hottest properties, though Allison would sit in the director's box at Gigg Lane telling the world – very vocally – how useless the player was. All this while his club were busy raising the funds to buy him!

Football was on a high after Alf Ramsey's England had won the World Cup, and there was a feel-good factor in Manchester, with United looking to make a serious challenge for the title again and City confident their new-look side would make a good impression on their return to Division One.

The Reds had Bobby Charlton, George Best and Denis Law, while the Blues had a swagger of their own with Mike Summerbee, Colin Bell and Neil Young among their number. In fact Harry Dowd and Bobby Kennedy were the only survivors from the previous campaign by the time of the landmark 75th league derby at Old Trafford. Both clubs had made reasonable starts, with United winning four and losing three of their opening seven games, while City had won two, drawn two and lost three. As ever, nothing was taken for granted, though United were the bookies' favourites.

The match started at a frantic pace as both sides made up for lost time and within 15 minutes there was an almighty kerfuffle in the City box with Denis Law in the thick of the melee. Six minutes later Law played a one-two with John Aston before rounding Dowd to slot the ball home. It proved to be the only goal of the game.

That win started a run that would take United to the top of the table, though they'd slipped to second by the time the teams met again at Maine Road the following January. It is worth noting that the 62,983 crowd was almost 1,000 more than the first derby – underlining that the Blues were still a major force in English football.

City, in 19th, were having trouble adapting to life in the top flight again and desperately needed something from this game – and they got it. The Blues kept Matt Busby's men at bay for 75 minutes before Bill Foulkes rose like a salmon to nod past City keeper Alan Ogley and seemingly win the game for United. But, with just seconds of normal time remaining, Bell's cross forced Nobby Stiles to take action to clear the ball and the England man planted a header firmly past Alex Stepney to send the City fans wild. It was a point gained rather than two lost for the Blues, though the opposite could be said for United who missed an opportunity to return to the top of the table. By the end of the season it didn't matter, with United claiming the title by four clear points from Nottingham Forest. Denis Law top-scored with 25 goals in all competitions, and few disagreed the Reds had been worthy winners. City lost just one of their remaining eight games to finish 15th, 10 points clear of the relegation zone.

Nobody, though, could have predicted what would happen the following season with United and City set to go head-to-head in one of the most exciting title battles the city had ever seen.

The Battle of Manchester

1967–1970

"There are times when you want to wring his neck. He hangs on to the ball when players have found better positions. Then out of the blue he wins you the match, and you know you're in the presence of someone special."

Paddy Crerand, Manchester United, on team-mate George Best, 1970

"It was a very simple team talk. All I used to say was: 'Whenever possible, give the ball to George Best'."

Sir Matt Busby

"No one in football could live with us. Between us we had it all. I charged into situations like a bull, full of aggressive ambition and contempt for anyone who might be standing in my way. And Joe came behind me, picking up the pieces, soothing the wounded and the offended with that vast charm."

Malcolm Allison

There was a feeling of optimism in each camp going into the 1967/68 campaign: United had proved they were the top dogs in the country and feared nobody, while City had a champagne swagger to their football that suggested they fancied themselves for silverware after a year of consolidation. Wayward winger Tony Coleman had been added to a nice blend of home-grown talent and prudent purchases, and for the derby on 30th September the Blues were determined to show their cross-city rivals that there were two teams in Manchester capable of winning the title.

With the wisdom instilled by Joe Mercer and the touch of arrogance added by Malcolm Allison, City, a point ahead going into this match, decided to go for broke and were ahead on five minutes through the brilliant Colin Bell who was looking a snip at the money City had paid Bury and was becoming more and more influential for the Blues. Bell then went close twice again but was denied by Alex Stepney who was just about keeping his team in the contest. But the champions were far from beaten and Bobby Charlton thumped home two goals before the break to give United a 2-1 lead they would carry through to the final whistle. It was a crushing defeat for Mercer's team but not one it couldn't recover from.

Down, but not out, City took a lot of heart from pushing the Reds so hard, and the Blues' management team identified the missing piece in their jigsaw when they paid £60,000 to Bolton Wanderers for the services of Francis (Franny) Lee.

Lee, a determined and physically strong striker, had a real edge to his game that would prove infectious to others, and he slotted into the team effortlessly. His style and confidence complemented the cultured play of Neil Young and the skills of Tony Coleman and Mike Summerbee on the wings. With Bell, Alan Oakes and Mike Doyle behind them it was a formidable side and City began to take opponents apart on a run that saw them go top going into March before a defeat to Leeds meant the Blues went into the return Manchester derby in third place, knowing a win could put them back joint top with Leeds. A win for United, however, and it would be the Reds who went top and, with a four-point gap, City's title challenge would surely falter.

A crowd of 63,004 packed into Old Trafford to see one of the most important battles between the Reds and the Blues for many years.

With only 38 seconds on the clock, United went ahead when George Best bamboozled Tony Book before tucking the ball past Ken Mulhearn for a quite incredible start. As Old Trafford celebrated the City players rolled their sleeves up determined not to let the opportunity of closing the gap on their rivals pass them by. Had the Reds scored again soon after, the course of history would have changed forever – but they didn't.

Gradually, inspired by Bell and Doyle, the Blues began to get on top and inevitably it was the brilliant Bell who levelled the scores as United wilted under a succession of City attacks. The Reds simply couldn't contain the Blues' marauding forwards and, when George Heslop nodded the Blues ahead from a Coleman free-kick, it was no more than Joe Mercer's men deserved. The Reds rallied, Law went close, but, when Francis Burns pulled down Bell in the box, Franny Lee stepped up to drill the penalty past Stepney to confirm a famous 3-1 win.

The victory put City level on points with United and Leeds as three teams entered the run-in with a real chance of winning the league, but it was the Blues who had the momentum and, by the final day of the season, a win would be enough to ensure the Division One trophy remained in Manchester, but this time in the blue half!

It was quite an incredible end to a thrilling season with, fittingly, the most dramatic 90 minutes of all still to come in a match that ebbed and flowed with more twists and turns than an Agatha Christie novel. City knew a victory at Newcastle United's St James' Park would guarantee them a first title since 1936, but a draw or loss and a Manchester United win over Sunderland and the Reds would remain champions. For both sets of fans it was unbearable and the week leading up to the final weekend saw both clubs big-up their chances, but only one team could triumph.

City believed this was their destiny with several kept results going their way at vital points of the season so, when Mike Summerbee put Joe Mercer's side 1-0 up, it seemed it was all meant to be. At least, that was, until Pop Robson equalized within 60 seconds! On the half-hour Neil Young restored City's lead, but again the hosts equalized within minutes through Jackie Sinclair.

News filtered through to Old Trafford but the Reds were choosing the wrong time to have a complete off day and were decidedly pedestrian against mid-table Sunderland.

Back in the northeast, events were about to take a decisive swing towards City who at last managed to get some daylight between themselves and Newcastle. Young and Francis Lee scored after the break to make it 4-2 and send the travelling masses wild, but John McNamee made it 4-3 with five minutes left to ensure around 20,000 Blues endured a nail-biting last few moments before the final whistle went and the victory was confirmed. Sunderland had won 2-0 at Old Trafford but it meant nothing – the Blues had won the title on merit rather than default.

As one half of the city celebrated, coach Malcolm Allison sent out a stark warning that City would go into the European Cup with a bold, attacking style that would frighten some of the clubs, who seemed only intent on avoiding defeat in the competition.

Allison spoke to the *Daily Mirror*, saying: "We will frighten them. Manchester City will not play in Europe the way European teams have played against Manchester United this season. They play as though they only want to avoid losing. We will attack in a way not seen since the old Real Madrid used to."

But that wasn't the end of major silverware heading to Manchester. United also had plenty to celebrate a few days later when they finally achieved Matt Busby's lifelong dream of winning the European Cup, beating Benfica at Wembley. Manchester was suddenly the football capital of the world.

For United, it was the end of one journey and, in many ways, the start of another. Matt Busby had been convinced his Babes were on their way to European greatness before Munich, so to survive the disaster after so nearly losing his life and then fashion another all-conquering side within a decade was testament to what an incredible man this was. The Reds had led 1-0 against the Portuguese side but were forced to eventually triumph in extra time, with three goals in six first-half minutes completing a 4-1 victory.

For the Reds, that was as good as it got for a number of years, but City's star was on the rise again and they had a squad of players who were hungry for more silverware. A summer break to recharge batteries was needed for all concerned, but City, unwisely, set off on a five-week tour of North America that was, in truth, the last thing they needed. By the resumption of league football Joe Mercer's side were a jaded bunch – and it quickly showed.

The first derby of the season ended in a colourless 0-0 draw, but the noticeable change in attitude is what lodged in minds of most who witnessed it, with United very much on the defensive and more than happy to play out the goalless draw.

Fortunately for Busby's cagey Reds City weren't at the races either and by the ninth game of the season the defending champions had slumped to second bottom of Division One – surely the Blues wouldn't repeat their only previous title success by being relegated the season after? City fans reckoned anything was possible!

The difference in the derby crowds around this time was invariably a few hundred but rarely more – further proof that there were now two superpowers in the city, and the Blues underlined their ascendency in the fixture by leaving Old Trafford with a hard-fought but thoroughly deserved 1-0 win courtesy of a Mike Summerbee goal on 39 minutes, created by some tenacious play from Mike Doyle. Both sides struck the woodwork but it was City who held on and claimed a morale-boosting victory amid some unpredictable league form.

By that point City knew there was no chance of retaining their title and, instead, had focused their efforts on the FA Cup, which they were progressing well in. Likewise, with United, who were also miles off the pace, the Reds were hopeful of defending the European Cup and reached the semi-finals, but they would ultimately lose to AC Milan to end the season without a trophy.

City, however, went on to win the FA Cup, with Mike Summerbee creating Neil Young's 24th-minute winner at Wembley against Leicester City. The Cup triumph rescued what had been a poor season for the Blues who finished in 13th, three places below United. It was scant consolation for the Reds who saw the end of an era, with Matt Busby retiring and becoming a director after a magnificent 24-year reign at Old Trafford.

Wilf McGuinness stepped in but little could he have realized he was stepping into the eye of a storm, with football in Manchester about to take a major swing towards City.

The 1969/70 season would see no fewer than five Manchester derbies, with two League Cup ties, one FA Cup clash and two league meetings; four of those games were played within a little over two months!

Once again, neither side started the season particularly well, but the Blues would still enjoy the campaign much more than United. The first league meeting underlined how things had changed in such a short space of time. Just two years earlier United had won the European Cup, now they were like frightened rabbits caught in the headlights as City systematically dismantled them. They called it one of the most one-sided derby matches ever – a defeat that the majority of the 63,000 people who witnessed it have never forgotten. The news reports commented on the "vast gulf between two ill-matched sides". City went into the match having failed to beat United at Maine Road since September 1959, but in good form in the league having lost just one of their previous 13 games.

Both sides were still attempting to get back on the rails having endured mediocre 1968/69 campaigns while, in City's case, defending the title and, in United's, the European Cup. While the Blues were riding high the Reds were clearly going through something of a transitional period.

With the teams due to meet again in a two-legged League Cup semi-final just a few weeks later, it was important to gain a psychological edge to take into those games. It was United who came desperately close to opening the scoring in the first minute, with Denis Law just failing to connect with John Aston's inviting ball across the box.

The Blues heeded the warning and effortlessly slipped up a gear from that moment on, though it wasn't until the 38th minute that the hosts finally went in front.

Neil Young had been fairly quiet up to that point but, when he received the ball within sight of goal, he feigned to cross but instead sent in a wicked curling drive that totally fooled Alex Stepney and flew into the back of the net.

City thought they'd gone two goals ahead on the break when Bell whipped in a superb cross that Lee volleyed home from 12 yards, but the referee ruled it out, saying he'd blown just before the ball hit the back of the net. With just one goal separating the sides at half-time the Reds could have been forgiven for thinking they had a good shot at clawing their way back into the match, but 10 minutes into the second half the peerless Colin Bell doubled City's advantage to make it 2-0 after a fine break out of defence and assist by Alan Oakes.

United's talismanic trio of Bobby Charlton, Law and George Best were powerless to prevent the continued tidal wave of attacks led by man-of-the-match Bell and, when the Blues went 3-0 up, courtesy of an own goal from the luckless David Sadler, the Kippax began to enjoy the occasion, safe in the knowledge that there was no way back for the Reds.

Mike Summerbee, Lee, Young and Bell had attacked from the front relentlessly, with a mixture of flair and aggression, and United had been overwhelmed. Oakes, Glyn Pardoe, Tony Book and, of course, Mike Doyle, played like men inspired. Nobody was about to take their foot off the gas, least of all the majestic Bell who scrambled home a fourth on 89 minutes from Young's unplayable cross to send Maine Road into ecstasy and complete United's dismal afternoon. The 4-0 scoreline in no way flattered Joe Mercer's side who showed the kind of form that had made them champions just 18 months earlier. And the only question City fans were asking was why couldn't their team turn on the style more often?

Less than three weeks later United had an early opportunity for revenge as the teams met again in the League Cup semi-final first leg. With the much-maligned competition's final now being played at Wembley there was a great demand to see both games and close to 120,000 would see Manchester's finest go head to head once again over two legs. Though the Reds fell behind on 13 minutes to a Colin Bell goal, Alex Stepney was on inspired form and kept United in the hunt until, finally, Bobby Charlton levelled the scores on 65 minutes. A first-leg draw would have been a fantastic result for the visitors but with less than two minutes remaining Francis Lee went down – as Francis Lee did from time to time – and the referee pointed to the spot. United argued Lee had dived but the City striker stepped up to bury the ball past Stepney to give the Blues a 2-1 advantage to take to Old Trafford.

The return game was equally frantic and after 15 minutes the Blues seemed to have one foot inside Wembley as Ian Bowyer reacted quickest after Neil Young's shot was parried by Stepney, but this tie was far from over.

Young United full-back Paul Edwards sent a long-range effort past City keeper Joe Corrigan and, after the break, Law sent the Stretford End wild with an aggregate equalizer to put the Reds 2-1 up on the night. But there was one final twist. With 83 minutes gone, the Blues won an indirect free-kick on the edge of United's box. Lee stepped up to take a shot, gambling that Stepney's instincts would make him try to save it – and he did, palming down the ball, and Mike Summerbee was on hand to fire home from close range. The irony was, if Stepney had left it and allowed Lee's shot to go into the net it would have been disallowed and the Reds would have been given a free-kick. A deflated United couldn't muster a response and City were back at Wembley less than a year after winning the FA Cup. The Blues were proving to be an excellent cup side and would go on to win the League Cup with a 2-1 win over West Brom courtesy of extra-time goals from Mike Doyle and Glyn Pardoe.

With fate pairing United and City together yet again in the FA Cup fourth round a few weeks later, it was perhaps inevitable that the Reds would finally triumph and Willie Morgan and Brian Kidd (2) comfortably eased the Old Trafford side into the fifth round.

There was still one more derby to go – the return league meeting at Old Trafford. United had turned their season into something approaching respectability by the time the 82nd league derby came around, but the great unpredictables that were Manchester City found their neighbours in generous mood on the day. Two David Sadler howlers ultimately did for United, with his first allowing Neil Young to sneak in and round Stepney who then brought him crashing down for a penalty. Lee, coolness personified, kept his nerve in front of a baying Stretford End to hammer the ball into the top right-hand corner to put his team ahead.

Sloppy play then resulted in an equalizer for United, with George Best wriggling past several tackles before feeding Willie Morgan, whose cross was only parried by an unsighted Corrigan, allowing Kidd a simple tap-in from close range just seven minutes later for his 17th of the season.

Sadler's hashed clearance before the break enabled Mike Doyle to nick in ahead of the United man, and realize a lifetime ambition, by scoring the winner at Old Trafford as he gleefully struck the ball home from 15 yards to give the Blues a second successive league double over United.

Though McGuinness' men finished two places higher than City the Blues went on to win the European Cup Winners' Cup with a 2-1 win over Polish giants Gornik Zabrze in Vienna to add to the League Cup and the four points they'd taken off United that season. It was clear who Manchester's top side was going into the new decade, and for the concerned followers of the Reds, there was no immediate end in sight to their misery.

Out with the Old

1970–1973

"It was a case of 'follow that!' and both teams tried to do exactly that as they each set off in pursuit of the title, safe in the knowledge that on their day both were more than capable of winning the league."

After so many years of stability United were about to slip outside of their comfort zone in more ways than one. Wilf McGuinness was struggling to steer his ageing side away from mid-table mediocrity and he needed a few high-profile successes if he was to convince a doubtful board that he was the man to take the club forward.

Similarly, at Maine Road, behind the scenes problems rumbled on with a new consortium, which included Peter Swales, bidding to remove the old guard who had run the club for so long. Malcolm Allison, not surprisingly, was in favour of new blood – who were keen to employ him as the new manager – while the more conservative Joe Mercer appeared happier with the men who had given him the opportunity to return to football after his illness. The situation would rumble on and clearly affect both clubs who would both end the season without any silverware.

At least the derby offered one set of fans some pleasure and, for the fifth time in six meetings in the league, it was the City fans who left Old Trafford in celebratory mood after watching their team record a fourth successive Division One win in the Reds' backyard.

The Blues, steady if not spectacular, were at the top of their game, while United never really got going, and Mike Doyle began the rout with another goal at the Stretford End. Colin Bell whipped in a perfect cross and Doyle out-jumped his marker to plant a world-class header past Jimmy Rimmer in off the far post. He celebrated as you might imagine a City fan celebrating the goal of his life: in front of a terrace full of United fans. Francis Lee then went on to score the first derby hat-trick in a decade with all his goals coming from open play – unusual for the penalty specialist. His first was a clever and instinctive finish from close range, his second was from a Summerbee cross, where he got just enough on the shot to see the ball trundle across the line, and his third was a splendid header from an Arthur Mann cross, earning himself £25 off Malcolm Allison who had backed against his striker getting five headed goals that season by sticking a fiver on at odds of 5/1! Lee's goal at Old Trafford was, of course, his fifth header that season but his wily coach was more than happy to cough up, commenting that Franny had now even started heading the ball with his eyes open!

Kidd pulled a late goal back, but it wasn't enough. The only black mark on the blue ribbon occasion was the late tackle by George Best that resulted in Glyn Pardoe breaking his leg. Pardoe needed an emergency operation to save his leg after an artery had become blocked but eventually recovered, though the City favourite was never quite the same player again.

Best apologized for the tackle and was visibly distraught after the game, with Malcolm Allison predicting it would take the United star "a long time to get over the incident".

United needed a quick fix to save their season, and a two-legged League Cup semi-final with Third Division Aston Villa offered them an excellent chance of another Wembley final. Yet Villa stunned the football world by first holding the Reds to a 1-1 draw at Old Trafford and then winning their home leg 2-1 to reach the final. That, coupled with a 4-4 draw with Derby, was enough to convince the United board to relieve McGuinness of his duties and bring Matt Busby back as manager until the end of the season.

City's only hope of silverware evaporated amid an injury crisis that couldn't have had worse timing. Robbed of Colin Bell, Mike Summerbee, Mike Doyle, Glyn Pardoe and Alan Oakes, City still put up a fight in the defence of the European Cup Winners' Cup, losing the first leg to Chelsea 1-0 at Stamford Bridge. Though a few of those stellar names returned for the semi-final second leg, City again lost 1-0 to crash out.

Considering the return Maine Road derby was on the final day of the campaign and the winners would guarantee finishing above the other, the 84th league meeting between the clubs was played almost like an exhibition match. Both sides came into the game on level pegging with 41 points apiece. City had the better goal difference so even a draw would be enough to take eighth spot but, with Sir Matt Busby announcing this would definitely be his last game in charge and the *This Is Your Life* crew springing a surprise on the Reds' legendary boss before kick-off, there was a feeling in the air that this was always going to be United's night. Besides, merely finishing above the other was viewed as a failure by both clubs who craved titles and trophies.

A demotivated and jaded-looking City were still missing Bell, Summerbee and Doyle – three constant thorns in the Reds' side in recent years – and an inexperienced Blues trailed 3-0 by half-time courtesy of Charlton, Best and Law; United were a clinical side on the day.

A disappointing crowd of 43,636 then saw City stage a second-half fight-back with Lee, Ian Mellor and Freddie Hill all scoring, though Best's headed second goal ultimately turned out to be the winner. United eased above City into eighth and the Blues slipped to 11th. It was the Reds' third successive higher-placed finish but neither side felt in celebratory mood after yet another flat season.

There was much more for the Mancunian masses to feel happy

about the following season. The first derby saw United back to somewhere near their best under new manager Frank O'Farrell, and on top of the table, while the Blues, under the tutelage of Joe Mercer for one final season, were in third just three points behind. After three years of doldrums in the league for both Manchester clubs it seemed the battle had reignited – and the meeting on 6th November 1971 proved to be one of the best derbies of all time.

O'Farrell had kept pretty much the same side that finished the previous season, but injected fresh impetus into his ageing troops, while City had brought in towering forward Wyn Davies from Newcastle United. For the Blues, Davies offered a different type of outlet. The big target man was soon put to good use and Franny Lee, in particular, was benefiting from Davies' lay-offs and flick-ons. In fact, the former Bolton striker had scored 12 goals in the first 15 league matches going into the derby and was in the form of his life.

O'Farrell lost Denis Law to injury before kick-off but had no hesitation in calling up 17-year-old Sammy McIlroy, who had been scheduled to play a youth match on the Saturday morning, as the Scot's replacement – it proved to be an inspired decision.

The Blues started the game with the confidence of a side who had won their previous eight home games in succession but United weathered the first half to finish the half intact at 0-0. The Reds came out for the second half with renewed belief and quickly established a 2-0 lead, thanks to the youthful exuberance of McIlroy, who showed ice cool nerves to out-fox the experienced Oakes and Book to tuck the ball home after fine work by Best. Brian Kidd made it 2-0 shortly after. The leaders looked well on their way to victory but City were made of sterner stuff and two quick goals turned the game on its head. First of all Franny Lee won and then converted a penalty to half the deficit and then Lee fed Bell who raced clear to round Alex Stepney and send Maine Road wild. But there was even better to come as Wyn Davies nodded a rampant City ahead – only for the referee to spot an infringement. With the home fans still giving the officials the bird United added fuel to the fire by regaining the lead when Alan Gowling deflected John Aston's bullet drive home. Now it was the visiting section who was in a state of ecstasy; however, there was one final twist still to come.

With the United fans begging referee Ray Tinkler to blow for full-time, Mike Summerbee found space to send in a thunderous drive towards the top corner. As Maine Road held its collective breath, Stepney somehow scrambled across to produce a stunning save, clawing what looked like a certain goal out for a corner. It was thrilling, edge of the seat stuff and the Blues' slender hopes resulted on the corner first finding a City head and, as far as the home support were concerned, then the back of the net. A hush fell as the ball was floated in, it looked like Stepney's all the way but, incredibly, he flapped at the cross and the ball fell to Summerbee who hammered it home to lift the roof off Maine Road. It was fantastic stuff and further proof that these two stylish Manchester clubs were still the nation's great entertainers.

It was a case of "follow that!" and both teams tried to do exactly that as they each set off in pursuit of the title, safe in the knowledge that on their day both were more than capable of winning the league.

Along the way, however, United dramatically imploded. A 2-1 win over Nottingham Forest was the Reds' fourth win on the trot after the derby, and sent O'Farrell's side five points clear. But the new United boss' honeymoon rapidly turned into a nightmare as an inexplicable set of results followed. Three successive draws against teams that should have been no more than cannon fodder followed and the confidence visibly drained from the league leaders. The points cushion and inability of those behind ensured United were still top by mid-January, but seven successive defeats saw them quickly plummet down the table. In all, they took just four points from a possible 22 – one of the club's worst runs ever.

With four games to go the Reds had slipped nine points behind City and were in eighth, while their sky blue neighbours were going full tilt for the Division One championship.

In fact, for many Reds followers, being able to halt City – who had to win at Old Trafford – would have rescued some pride back, but it wasn't to be.

The Blues had endured a minor blip of their own, taking just one point from a possible six going into the derby and losing pole position. Many blamed the £200,000 purchase of Rodney Marsh as part of the dip in form but, in truth, a run of poor results could happen at any point, so it is perhaps unfair to single Marsh out as the reason.

Nonetheless, the Blues stormed back to form at Old Trafford and, despite going behind to a second-half Martin Buchan goal, hit back within 60 seconds to level through Franny Lee's header to suddenly rediscover their sparkle. Five minutes later and Lee had his 32nd goal of the season, drilling home Summerbee's tempting cross to give his side a 2-1 lead. Rounding off a superb win was substitute Marsh who replaced Mike Doyle and put the result beyond all doubt when he coolly finished Bell's pass to ensure two points and put City firmly back in the title race.

Level on points with Derby County, but with an inferior goal average, City still had to play the Rams on the final day – all Joe Mercer's side needed to do was hope that Liverpool and Leeds (both with a game in hand in third and fourth) lost, while seeing off Coventry City and Ipswich Town who were both in the lower half of the table.

Somehow the Blues blew it, taking a point in total from both games. City did beat Derby 2-0 on the final day but needed several results to go their way from the teams beneath them who still had one or two games to play. The Blues remained top for an agonizing week before Derby and then Leeds both won to climb ahead, and the title dream was over. Brian Clough's Derby won one of the closest championships for years and City finished fourth, just one point behind and dreaming about what could have been had they not failed to win five of their last eight games.

Joe Mercer stepped down after seven fantastic years in charge at Maine Road and Malcolm Allison finally got his wish of becoming the top man. Mercer left for Coventry as City entered a new era. After such a dramatic season fans of both sides, emotionally exhausted, wondered, what next?

Law-abiding Citizen

1973–1976

"We were gutted the year we got United relegated – while they were on the fixture list, it was a guaranteed four points."

Mike Doyle, 1999

"All his life Denis Law has loved goals. That one, even though it was a bit special, he hated."

Frank McGhee, *Daily Mirror*

City were back to their unpredictable best – or worst – during the 1972/73 campaign and were brilliant at home, abysmal away. United, by contrast, were equally inept at Old Trafford, and elsewhere, and were rooted to the foot of the table by the time the 87th Manchester league derby arrived. With the Blues winning seven of their nine games at Maine Road up to that point, the Reds' stock was at an all-time low going into the game, notwithstanding the fact that the form book was generally disregarded for these games.

A bad-tempered affair ensued and it was City who would triumph, teeth bared for all to see, in a war of attrition in which the modern-day game would have seen red cards aplenty. Though both teams were guilty of over-the-top aggressive tackling, it was clear from the first 50-50 challenge that Malcolm Allison had pumped his team up and they were taking no prisoners.

The Blues were ahead as early as seven minutes when a mistake by Stepney let in Bell who made no mistake and, as the tackles continued to fly in, the Reds just about clung on for dear life. In fact they remained just a goal behind until the latter stages when Bell doubled his, and City's, tally and then saw his fierce shot diverted home by Buchan to complete a comprehensive 3-0 victory.

The Reds seemed to be down and out and, within a month, after a humiliating 5-0 defeat at the hands of Crystal Palace, Frank O'Farrell was sacked.

City, too, parted company with Allison who discovered managing was a totally different beast to coaching. Amid rumours of disharmony and poor form he quit Maine Road and became boss of Crystal Palace. United brought in the larger-than-life Tommy Docherty, while City promoted within, going from the flash and brash Big Mal to the understated calmness of coach Johnny Hart.

Neither new boss could inspire their troops to anything approaching an entertaining display as the Old Trafford derby ended 0-0. Docherty had steadied the Reds' defence and steered them well clear of relegation, while City drifted aimlessly in mid-table.

The 1973/74 campaign promised more transition and, perhaps, mediocrity. Denis Law had returned to City on a shock free transfer, with Hart convincing him to have one last hurrah, while George Best played his last game for United on 1st January 1974. Disenchanted he quit Old Trafford for good. The maverick Northern Irishman had courted more media attention than any other footballer on the planet and was the first real playboy of the modern game. But Best, tired of the direction United were headed, would later claim: "It had nothing to do with women and booze, car crashes or court cases. It was purely football. Losing wasn't in my vocabulary. When the wonderful players I had been brought up with – Charlton, Law, Crerand, Stiles – went into decline, United made no real attempt to buy the best replacements. I was left struggling among fellas who should not have been allowed through the door. It sickened me that we ended up being just about the worst team in the First Division."

United's holy trinity of Charlton, Best and Law was now confined to history and, soon, the Reds' time in Division One would also end.

Both teams had already played 30 league games by the time the first derby of the season took place at Maine Road, and this brutal affair was to prove memorable for all the wrong reasons. The Blues, now managed by Ron Saunders, who had also guided his team to the League Cup final (where they lost 2-1 to Wolves), were patchy at best, while United were attempting to bully their way out of a relegation battle. City, who still included the feisty talents of Summerbee, Doyle and Tommy Booth, were more than a match for the Reds' roughhouse tactics and seemed to enjoy the ruck that followed. As each bone crunching tackle went in one after the next referee Clive Thomas had trouble keeping up with events and, eventually, decided enough was enough, showing a red card to United's Lou Macari and City's Mike Doyle. Ironically, the pair claimed their latest tussle had been a misunderstanding and refused to leave the pitch, leaving Thomas with no other option than to take both sides off to sort the situation out. When the players did re-emerge it was minus Macari and Doyle and others could, and perhaps should, have followed. With the bad feeling inevitably spilling on to the terraces, it was a relief for all concerned when the referee blew for full-time with the teams sharing a 0-0 draw. Crowd trouble was a regular feature of derby day, with hooliganism on the increase and the passion of a derby game a breeding ground for loutish behaviour.

The return game was played just six weeks later and could not have been any more dramatic if a Hollywood director had scripted it.

The maths were simple – a defeat for United and they were relegated. Their situation already looked hopeless but, while there was still hope, they had to at least try to get a win, which would give them a glimmer of hope. For City, now under caretaker manager Tony Book following Ron Saunders' sacking, this was a chance to send their neighbours down.

As yet another feisty derby seemingly headed for a goalless draw – enough to condemn Tommy Docherty's side to Division Two – City launched what would be one final attack. Bell fed Lee who drilled a low cross into the six-yard box where – who else? – Denis Law was waiting, and his predatory instincts overruled his heart with a superb back-heel that would be his last kick in professional football. It was his ninth goal in 22 starts for City and easily his best but, as the realization sunk in that it was he, "the King" of Old Trafford, who had effectively confirmed United's relegation to Division Two, Law visibly wilted. He did not celebrate, despite being urged to by his City team-mates, and was immediately substituted, visibly distraught. A pitch invasion followed, but was dealt with, and play resumed for five minutes before a mass invasion stopped the game. Amid disgraceful scenes the referee took the players back to the safety of the dressing rooms. This time the United fans wouldn't budge and, despite pleas from Sir Matt Busby, the referee David Smith took the wise decision of effectively abandoning the game with the 1-0 result standing. News had filtered through that Birmingham and Southampton had won their games so United would have been relegated regardless of the result.

Manchester United had gone from being champions of Europe to Division Two also-rans in the space of six seasons and were out of the top flight for the first time in 36 years. It was a devastating blow for the Reds, who also now had the problem of a sizeable hooligan following many clubs in the top flight were glad to see the back of – at least for 12 months.

Reporting in the *Daily Mirror*, Frank McGhee, the "Voice of Sport" said: "I have seldom seen a more poignant moment in sport captured on television than the expression of Law's face after he'd scored the goal that sealed his old team's tomb," wrote McGhee.

"And I have never seen anyone being consoled rather than congratulated for scoring. All his life Denis Law has loved goals. That one, even though it was a bit special, he hated.

"Does anyone really doubt that if Law had not been taken off and substituted he risked being attacked by some of the filth that spilled over on to the pitch? Once there wouldn't have been a dry eye in neutral country at United's relegation. Now there isn't a wet one. Perhaps their fans will think about that."

Tommy Docherty, who had almost steered United to safety, remained in the hot-seat and he concocted a more-than-decent squad after making several prudent signings and bringing a number of home-grown youngsters through. The green shoots of recovery were there for all to see as United and City were paired for a third-round League Cup tie at Old Trafford where a Gerry Daly penalty saw the Reds through, giving United fans a cause for optimism about the immediate future, and a victory that gave them unexpected bragging rights for a while. They were ultimately knocked out at the semi-final stage by Norwich, but they had proved they weren't a million miles from where they wanted to be.

The truth was, the cup mattered little: United wanted their Division One status back. After just one season in the wilderness they got it winning the second tier at a canter and taking the title. The Blues had given Tony Book the manager's job on a permanent basis and had begun their own rebuilding programme with Asa Hartford and Joe Royle arriving at Maine Road. Francis Lee had been sold to Derby – probably a couple of years too soon – as former team-mate Book made one or two difficult decisions. The season was steady but not spectacular.

Dave Watson was also added for the 1975/76 campaign and youngsters Peter Barnes, son of City great Ken, and Kenny Clements were promoted to the senior side as Book continued to build a new side.

By the time the teams resumed their league battle United had rediscovered their swagger and verve and arrived at Maine Road in second place having topped the table for most of the campaign so far. It would be a largely enjoyable season for both clubs, who would each return to Wembley later in the season, and the 91st derby was a cracker, with a memorable first half. City went ahead through Jimmy Nicholl lobbing his own keeper as Royle closed in, but the Reds hit back immediately with two goals in the space of two minutes, courtesy of David McCreery and Lou Macari. While the United fans were still celebrating Royle then levelled the score in City's next attack – it was exhilarating, breath-taking stuff and, with barely half an hour played, the score was 2-2. The game could not possibly continue at such a frenetic pace and it didn't, with no further goals scored and the points shared. There may have been no outright winner but it proved the Manchester derby was alive and kicking after its brief hiatus.

If United needed bringing down to earth, however, City were just the club to do it and, when the League Cup again pitted the Manchester giants together, it was normal service resumed as the Blues picked apart the Reds in emphatic style; but the victory came at a terrible price for City.

The Blues roared out of the blocks and were ahead within the first minute through Dennis Tueart, but then came a moment that not just impacted on this game but also the rest of the season. As Colin Bell surged towards the United box Martin Buchan's mistimed tackle brought the Blues' talisman crashing to the ground. The seriousness of the injury to Bell's knee quickly became apparent with the England midfielder clearly in agony. The extent of the problem wouldn't become clear until later but, in the meantime, Tommy Booth replaced Bell and the game continued. Asa Hartford and Tueart scored either side of the half-hour mark to all but seal the tie before the break. Joe Royle added a fourth in the second half to complete a 4-0 rout and seemingly dent the Reds' early-season confidence. As it was, United quickly got back to winning ways and continued their title assault.

For City, the diagnosis on Bell's knee was not good; such was the screening at the time it wasn't deemed as bad as it actually was, though he was side-lined for the next five months at least.

The Blues adapted well in his absence, however, with Ged Keegan and Paul Power doing sterling work between them, particularly during the League Cup run which would see City end their six-year wait for silverware by beating Newcastle 2-1 at Wembley in the final.

For United, there was the prospect of a first league and FA Cup double – the Holy Grail of English football – and, but for having a blip at exactly the wrong time, they may well have gone on to do exactly that.

With three games to go the Reds were challenging strongly for the title and had reached the FA Cup final, where they would face Division Two side Southampton. Yet, defeats to Stoke and Leicester in the league and a shock defeat to the Saints, meant a season that had promised so much ended without any trophies at all, though there was still the final game of the campaign to come – a derby at home to City which the Reds could at least enjoy winning 2-0. Two goals in four second-half minutes just after the break from Gordon Hill and Sammy McIlroy gave the near-60,000 capacity crowd a lift just days after losing the Cup final. City, who looked ready for their holidays, offered little in a disappointing 90 minutes.

Two Tribes

1976–1979

"Bell returned as half-time substitute against Newcastle United, at a packed Maine Road, and received a standing ovation that lasted for several minutes as he ran out."

There was no let-up of intensity in the Manchester rivalry during the 1976/77 campaign but, though it would be City who finished higher in the league, it was a Reds' derby double that perhaps robbed the Blues of a third Division One title.

Tony Book had fashioned a solid, balanced and attractive side that seemed more than capable of challenging to win the league. Brian Kidd, the former United striker, had been purchased from Arsenal for £100,000 and the buoyant Blues went into the September Maine Road derby in great heart top of the table and unbeaten in their opening six games.

United, too, had started really well and had lost just once in what promised to be a closely-fought game. Tueart, again, was proving a thorn in the Reds' side and it was the former Sunderland forward who sent the City fans wild after just seven minutes. United struck back on 22 minutes when Nicholl's cross found Steve Coppell who spun and struck the ball past Joe Corrigan for a deserved equalizer. Substitute David McCreery then gave the Reds the advantage before the break, but the game was still finely balanced and there was everything to play for. Then, a moment of controversy as Paul Power's shot was cleared off the line by Buchan with the City players claiming it had crossed the line only for the referee to wave play on. A couple of minutes later and Gerry Daly cracked home United's third, from a Gordon Hill cross, to put the outcome beyond doubt. It was the perfect riposte from the Reds.

City soon recovered and continued their quest for glory, losing just one of their next 17 league games, while United briefly topped the table after their Maine Road victory before plummeting down to 14th (and went as low as 17th) but, showing unpredictability almost exclusively saved for the Blues, they then went on a fantastic run and were in red-hot form. By the time of the Old Trafford derby the Reds were in fifth, six points behind leaders Liverpool, while City were in second, just a point off the top.

As with the first meeting, however, it was United who would triumph with a high-octane attacking display that put City on the back foot from the off. The Blues simply couldn't get out of their own half often enough to repel the wave of attacks, and there was an air of inevitability about United's opening goal. Stuart Pearson struck the Reds ahead first and Gordon Hill added a second seven minutes later as the Reds' first-half dominance paid dividends. There was more to come, too, when Coppell made it 3-0 after the break, and only an outstanding performance by Joe Corrigan prevented a far heavier defeat for the title hopefuls. A late Tueart goal was scant consolation for the travelling fans who knew only too well that this defeat was a hammer blow that would take some recovering from.

In a reverse of the previous campaign the title challengers ended up with nothing – City would finish runners-up to Liverpool by just one point – while United brought home a trophy after beating Liverpool 2-1 in the FA Cup final. It would be Tommy Docherty's final act as boss, after a breach of club ethics rendered him unemployed. City were left dreaming about what might have been: the two derby defeats produced no points whereas a draw in each would have seen the Blues crowned champions. Few realized it would be more than three decades before City again finished so high, as United gradually began to dominate football in Manchester, then England and eventually Europe.

For the 1977/78 campaign City felt one more player just might make the difference between finishing runners-up and winning the title. Mick Channon was bought from Southampton for a club record £300,000. Yet again both clubs had made an impressive start and came into the game joint top on seven points, with City having a better goal difference and sitting in first.

Still smarting from last season's derby double disappointment the Blues were in no mood to let United repeat that feat and were soon ahead thanks to Brian Kidd's pile-driver free-kick on 14 minutes. The former United striker added a second before the break to make it 2-0 and showed none of the regret former United team-mate Law had shown when scoring against his former employers. There was no let-up after half-time either, with Tony Book's men retaining the same intensity and gradually wearing down the Reds' resistance, until Channon wrapped up the points on 79 minutes with a clever low drive that gave Stepney no chance. Recent tradition demanded a consolation goal be scored and Jimmy Nicholl duly obliged with a fierce low drive before full-time. It was a third successive 3-1 derby scoreline, but it was also payback for the Blues who had good cause to feel pleased with themselves.

Mixed form plagued both sides during the autumn by which time the Reds had added Leeds United pair Gordon McQueen and Joe Jordan to their ranks. City had won just four of their previous 13 games going into the Christmas period, but the Boxing Day return of the inspirational Colin Bell, who had battled back to passable fitness against all the odds, was about to kick-start the Blues' title challenge.

Bell returned as half-time substitute against Newcastle United, at a packed Maine Road, and received a standing ovation that lasted for several minutes as he ran out. And what a fillip it proved to be for Book's side who, after drifting aimlessly towards mid-table, suddenly found their belief and confidence again. City won that game 4-0 and then won their next six league games to move from ninth to second in the table.

The Reds, now managed by Dave Sexton who had replaced Tommy Docherty, were having a distinctly average season in mid-table, so the Blues were the slight favourites when the teams met again at Old Trafford in March. As ever, the formbook was tossed out of the window as Sexton's side went 2-0 up thanks to two Gordon Hill penalties. As the majority of the 58,398 fans taunted the away section, the Blues staged a stirring fight-back with Kidd, again, playing a pivotal role. First he fired in a powerful drive that Stepney could only parry and Peter Barnes was on hand to stab the ball home. Then, just a minute later, a shell-shocked home defence was breached again as Hartford put Kidd clear and the former Stretford End favourite made no mistake to earn City a point.

The Blues would finish in fourth after a poor finish of just three wins in the last 13 games, seven of which had been drawn. United finished in 10th, 10 points behind their neighbours in what had been a flat season all round.

The 1978/79 season was at odds with the past few years for City who were about to enter a period of turbulence that almost came out of nowhere. After a solid start to the campaign United won the first meeting at Old Trafford with an 89th-minute Joe Jordan goal settling a rather uninspiring game. The Blues appeared to be losing their way and a team packed with England and Scotland internationals just couldn't get going. Book's men embarked on a disastrous league run of six draws and seven defeats and, by mid-January, looked as though they may end the season by being relegated. Malcolm Allison returned as chief coach but seemed to be running first-team affairs. For Tony Book it was an awkward situation, with his mentor effectively now his No.2 – it was never going to work. A gut-wrenching 3-0 home defeat to United a few weeks later suggested the Blues needed more than Big Mal's Second Coming to save their season. Two goals from Steve Coppell and a fine third by Andy Ritchie only served to underline the different paths the two teams were now taking.

United finished ninth and City managed to collect enough points to finish 15th. The Reds at least had a third FA Cup final in four years to look forward to, and were staring defeat in the face after going 2-0 down to Arsenal in the first half. Despite two dramatic late goals from McQueen and McIlroy pulling the Reds level, Alan Sunderland scored again in the last minute to clinch the trophy for the Gunners to complete what had been quite an amazing game.

A Kick Up the Eighties

1979–1982

"United topped the table as they ran out at Maine Road in November 1979 for the last meeting of the Seventies, while the Blues hovered above the relegation zone; but if history had taught us anything about the Manchester derby, it was to always expect the unexpected…"

Revolution or evolution? With Malcolm Allison now in control and Tony Book taking on the role of general manager the changes at Maine Road over the summer ensured that the Blues grabbed all the headlines, though not necessarily for reasons their supporters were pleased about. Allison decided a fresh approach was needed at all levels and embarked on a cull of seasoned professionals such as Brian Kidd, Dave Watson, Asa Hartford, Peter Barnes, Gary Owen and Mick Channon that defied logic. Dennis Tueart had left the previous January, Mike Doyle had joined Stoke and Colin Bell had finally hung up his boots, so the City starting XI that finished against United eight months earlier contained 10 new names; United's showed five changes.

With so many experienced players exiting Maine Road Allison brought in a mixture of youth and promising talent as well as paying extravagant prices for Wolves' Steve Daley and Preston's Michael Robinson – a combined fee of £2.2m for two unproven players was a massive gamble. Tommy Caton, a 16-year-old central-defender, was promoted to the senior side as were reserve players Dave Bennett and Tony Henry. United went for proven quality by paying £850,000 for Chelsea's Ray Wilkins. For the neutrals, it was fascinating but City fans had good reason to believe Allison was reckless with his purchases and flippant with some of the players he forced out. If it paid off it would be his greatest coup yet but, if it failed, it would almost certainly cost him his job.

United topped the table as they ran out at Maine Road in November 1979 for the last meeting of the Seventies, while the Blues hovered above the relegation zone; but if history had taught us anything about the Manchester derby it was to always expect the unexpected.

Steve Daley, struggling to come to terms with being Britain's most expensive footballer, was industrious and clever and the Blues just had that bit more about them. After a goalless first 45 minutes the breakthrough goal was always going to prove vital and it was Tony Henry who grabbed it by reacting quickly to a loose ball in the box to beat Gary Bailey. The Blues rose in stature and Robinson drilled home a second 10 minutes from time to seal a very welcome 2-0 win for City. Unfortunately the result merely papered over cracks that could not be filled and that was as good as it got for the Blues in what turned out to be an utterly miserable – and at times embarrassing – campaign, which peaked in the mud of Halifax Town's the Shay, where the Blues were dumped out of the FA Cup by the Fourth Division strugglers. It was an all-time low for City fans and there would be little to cheer for in the coming seasons.

Like a heavy drinker hitting the bottle, the Blues again turned to the chequebook to try to lift spirits. Crowd idol Dennis Tueart had returned to Maine Road from New York Cosmos, while Kevin Reeves had joined the £1m club when he signed from Norwich.

The Reds were having a good season and were in second by the time City visited Old Trafford for the historic 100th league Manchester derby. Though six points off leaders Liverpool there was still hope that the gap could be closed, especially with a home game against the Merseysiders still to come. The Blues were still anxiously looking over their shoulders at the relegation trapdoor, sitting just five points ahead of the third-bottom club and in the middle of an awful 13-match run without a victory. Three goals in seven games also suggested City wouldn't be troubling Gary Bailey that much and, during a truly forgettable game, Mickey Thomas' winner shortly after the break proved enough to give United a 1-0 win. Dave Sexton's side finished two points behind champions Liverpool, while City managed to win three of their last four games to ensure survival in 17th spot.

Six months later and the teams were back at Old Trafford for the 1980/81 derby. Allison's tenure at Maine Road looked set to end with no wins in the first seven games meaning, in effect, his side had won just three times in 27 games. Second bottom, the football was poor and the team were seemingly lacking direction. United, for their sins, were being accused of playing negatively and had managed just nine goals in seven games. The match itself was a story of City's dogged refusal to throw the towel in more than anything else. The chips were certainly down but it appeared the Blues still had the belly for a fight.

Steve Coppell scored his fifth derby goal on 30 minutes but City equalized on the stroke of half-time through a thumping Kevin Reeves header to send 10,000 travelling fans wild. United restored their lead on 72 minutes through a cracking Arthur Albiston strike from 25 yards. It seemed that would be enough to secure both points and pile yet more misery on the Blues but, just as they had done in the first period, City scored at the end of the half with Roger Palmer's predatory instincts there for all to see once again with a goal on 89 minutes that silenced a baying Stretford End.

The result was a great one for Allison but it proved to be no more than a stay of execution and three more losses followed, convincing the board to finally sack him and Tony Book. It had been coming for some time and something had to be done before it was too late. Rooted to the foot of the table City brought in Norwich boss John Bond and things quickly picked up.

United were still drawing too many games and the gap between the teams – which had been 10 points in mid-October – was now down to four. By the end of John Bond's first Manchester derby it would be down to two.

With the Reds drawing more than half of their 30 games there was discontent among the Old Trafford faithful indicating that perhaps it was time for Dave Sexton to move on. He had little or no rapport with the fans or the media and it seemed only a matter of time before he followed Malcolm Allison out of Manchester.

In contrast, City had won 10 and drawn four of Bond's first 17 league games and, if you added five domestic cup wins out of seven, it was the form of title contenders – a remarkable turnaround influenced by Bond's astute transfer acquisitions of Gerry Gow, Bobby McDonald and Tommy Hutchison, all bought for a combined fee of less than £500,000. Having narrowly lost to Liverpool in the League Cup semi-final just days earlier, City were also in the FA Cup quarter-finals, where they would face Everton.

It seemed Bond could do no wrong and he watched his side continue their excellent progress on all fronts as Steve MacKenzie cracked home what would be the only goal of the game on the hour mark to send the blue masses in the 50,114 crowd home with smiles as wide as a Cheshire cat's.

United had been poor and colourless and their expensive recent signing Garry Birtles – purchased for £1.2m from Nottingham Forest – had gone yet another game without scoring a goal (his 14th in a row since arriving). In later years, the joke in Manchester was that when political prisoner Terry Waite was released by his captors in Lebanon after four years of incarceration, the first thing he asked was, "Has

Birtles scored yet?"

City couldn't quite cap their amazing rollercoaster of a season off with a trophy after losing the Centenary FA Cup final to Spurs in a Wembley replay, while Sexton was shown the door at Old Trafford after failing to impress the United fans or board with his conservative style of football. It seemed the pendulum had swung back in the Blues' favour.

United identified the man they wanted to put the bling back into their football, and West Brom boss Ron Atkinson arrived at Old Trafford with a penchant for gold jewellery, an all-year-round tan and a reputation for swashbuckling football – it was a marriage made in heaven. By the 103rd derby at Maine Road in October 1981 he had brought in John Gidman, Frank Stapleton and Remi Moses – plus his former skipper at West Brom, Bryan Robson, signed for a British record fee of £1.8m.

City, too, had bought big with Trevor Francis becoming the club's third £1m signing in three years. Francis wasn't available for this game but Robson made his debut and made an instant impact in a match that eventually ended 0-0.

Both Manchester clubs were still in contention for the title when they met at Old Trafford four months later. City had hit the summit going into the New Year but their form had fallen away slightly by the derby. United were only four points off leaders Southampton, with the Blues another four points adrift. United had to win to keep the pressure on the Saints, but Reeves headed City ahead and only Kevin Moran's brave header earned Big Ron's side a disappointing 1-1 draw. Dropping two points a blow to the Reds' title aspirations and they eventually finished third – with a club record 78 points thanks to the new three points for a win rule – with City 20 points further behind in 10th. The Blues seemed to have stagnated somewhat under Bond, but few could have predicted the drama the 1982/83 season was about to bring...

The Reds March On

1982–1989

"Howard Kendall worked things out very quickly. Good luck to him for seeing the problems before I did. It's a club where you can be the world's greatest and the world's worst within a few days."

Mel Machin, shortly after his sacking from Manchester City, 1990

United were flying in 1982/83, while City were steadily imploding. There was a shortage of quality in the blue ranks, with cut-price signings such as David Cross and Peter Bodak replacing players like Trevor Francis and Tommy Hutchison. The Reds, by contrast, had a squad packed with internationals.

Big Ron's side would challenge on three different fronts and topped the table for the 105th derby, while City were holding their own in eighth. It had been eight years since the Blues had managed to win at Old Trafford but, when goals from Tueart and Cross gave City a surprise 2-0 half-time lead, that statistic looked set to end. However, United were far from finished and staged a rousing second-half performance to earn a 2-2 draw following a Frank Stapleton brace. By early November City had overtaken United and moved into second place but would then dramatically drop into free-fall.

A 4-0 FA Cup fourth-round defeat to Brighton saw John Bond quit his post at Maine Road and assistant boss John Benson took over the reins in a caretaker capacity.

City fans had watched their neighbours reach the League Cup final and reach the last eight of the FA Cup, as well as challenge for the title, and the 5th of March return at Maine Road made things even worse for them. Despite Kevin Reeves nodding City ahead Stapleton repeated his two-goal salvo once again to seal a 2-1 win. The Blues steadily slipped down the table until a 1-0 defeat to Luton on the final day of the campaign saw City lose their top-flight status for the first time in 17 years. It was devastating for the Blues' fans who then had to watch United win the FA Cup against the side who had perhaps started the rot – Brighton and Hove Albion – and go on and achieve a third-place league finish. For the next two seasons there would be no Manchester derby or even a sniff of one.

In 1983/84 City brought in former Celtic boss Billy McNeill to try to take them back to the top flight, but he would narrowly miss guiding the Blues up with a fourth-place finish. United also finished fourth as the title continued to elude Ron Atkinson's talented side, but in 1984/85 City won promotion back to Division One. United finished fourth again and added another FA Cup success to their growing roll of honour after Norman Whiteside's goal proved enough for 10-man United (Kevin Moran having become the first player to see red in a final) to beat Everton 1-0.

Both teams had changed beyond recognition from their last meeting. City had lost long-serving goalkeeper Joe Corrigan and fielded a completely different 11 from the team that had lost 2-1 in 1983. The Reds had six players from that game but had added Gordon Strachan and home-grown talents, such as Norman Whiteside, Mark Hughes and Paul McGrath, were now staples of the team that had made their best ever start to a season. For both sets of fans there was the curious sight of Sammy McIlroy in sky blue and Peter Barnes in red, with the former crowd favourites for each team now plying their trade on the opposite sides of the city.

United had won all seven of their games, while City had made a less spectacular but steady start putting eight points on the board and settling in mid-table. This game went to form and United won at a canter, looking stronger in every department in a comprehensive 3-0 win. Bryan Robson put United ahead from the penalty spot and goals from full-backs Arthur Albiston and Mike Duxbury completed the Blues' misery.

The tables had turned slightly for the return fixture. Robson, the Reds' Captain Fantastic, was proving injury prone and was absent again and it was announced star striker Mark Hughes would be allowed to move on during the summer with a deal with Barcelona in place. Atkinson had also brought in a number of questionable signings including Peter Davenport, Terry Gibson, Colin Gibson and Chris Turner.

City had enjoyed a solid return to the top flight and were safe in mid-table by the time they travelled to Old Trafford, while United, who had won their first 10 games in a row and had a 10-point lead at the top, had won only nine of their next 23 matches and were now trailing Everton by three points with the momentum very much with the Merseysiders.

Still, out of sorts or not, Big Ron's men were expected to complete the double over their neighbours and most of the 51,274 gathered to see exactly that – and it seemed as though they would leave happy with Colin Gibson giving United an early lead and Gordon Strachan doubling their advantage from the penalty spot after the break. The Blues kept plugging away and could sense the anxiety emanating off the terraces, knowing one goal could really crank up the pressure. It came after 71 minutes when Clive Wilson's low diving header put City right back in contention. With the United fans screaming at their team to up the ante and the Blues pouring forward at every opportunity, Arthur Albiston chased a ball back towards his goal with Paul Simpson hot on his heels – it was enough pressure to force the United defender to hit a poorly judged back pass that Chris Turner had no chance of stopping. A 2-2 draw and, eventually, a fourth placed finish, was deemed as failure by the Reds' board and

Atkinson's tenure was suddenly under threat – he needed to get off to a flyer in August or face the consequences. City finished 15th, and considering the squad McNeill had at his disposal, that wasn't a bad showing at all.

Just six games into the 1986/87 campaign and City were again looking for a new boss, with Billy McNeill quitting his post. Jimmy Frizzell stepped up from his role as No.2 but, by the time the Manchester tribes got together for the 109th derby, both teams were in the relegation zone. The quality of the match merited two teams doing so poorly, with Frank Stapleton's 50th-minute header putting United ahead, but Mick McCarthy sent in an equally thumping header a minute later to bring City level to complete the scoring.

There would be a bonus meeting in the FA Cup third round in January, and Norman Whiteside's goal proved enough to send the Reds into the next round in a dull affair at Old Trafford.

Though this didn't do much for either side's plight, and interest in the game seemed at an all-time low, the crowd of just 32,440 was the worst City derby crowd for an astonishing 83 years. The fact that the game had become the first derby to be shown live on terrestrial television had to be taken into account, but it was 16,000 down on the previous season.

Ten days after the derby the United board decided they needed a change of direction and sacked Atkinson, bringing in Aberdeen boss Alex Ferguson as his replacement. The new manager guided United towards mid-table safety, while City's survival was on a knife-edge two points above the bottom three. This was a poor derby for the neutral, won by United, thanks to an own goal by Nicky Reid on 60 minutes and a killer second from Bryan Robson before the end. It was a pale imitation of the derbies of yesteryear and the defeat for City came during a run of 13 games without a win, resulting in a second relegation in four years.

Again, City would take two years to return to Division One, with new boss Mel Machin blooding a crop of exciting youngsters during the Blues' rehabilitation. Alex Ferguson almost guided United to the title in his second season, finishing second to an exceptional Liverpool side who had dominated the decade. The 11th-place finish of 1988/89 was not so warmly received and, already, questions were being asked about Ferguson's ability to make the Reds a major force again. After derby No.111 those questions had become major doubts as City recorded their first win over United in eight years.

Ferguson had fashioned a new-look Reds side that included Viv Anderson, Mike Phelan, Gary Pallister, Paul Ince and Brian McClair, while newly-promoted City had brought prolific marksman Clive Allen in from Bordeaux and Ian Bishop from Bournemouth for less than £2m. Though United had started marginally better and were in mid-table, the Blues were third from bottom with four defeats in their opening six games. Fans of both teams in the 43,246 crowd could be forgiven for having low expectations on the day but few could have imagined the 90 minutes that would unravel before their eyes.

City had one of those days where everything they tried came off, and memories of a depressing decade were wiped out almost in an instant with a stunning victory against the old enemy. Crowd trouble – a familiar part of derby day – broke out, after a few minutes, in the North Stand and the teams were taken off the pitch while order was restored. Those few moments seemed to re-focus City's desire and it was the Blues who came out and tore into United after the restart; two goals in a minute suggested it was going to be Mel Machin's side's day.

First David Oldfield smashed home David White's clever pull-back and then Trevor Morley followed up Paul Lake's shot to make it 2-0. Maine Road erupted and United were being torn to shreds as Oldfield found Bishop with a perfect cross and the City midfielder's diving header put the hosts 3-0 up at the break. Even with that three-goal cushion City fans were edgy when a spectacular Mark Hughes volley made it 3-1 within a few moments of the restart, but they needn't have worried because, on the hour, Lake laid on Oldfield to make it 4-1. There was still one magnificent goal to come and it arrived shortly after as Bishop set White away down the right and the City winger's first-time cross was met on the full by the head of Andy Hinchcliffe who powered a header past Jim Leighton to make it 5-1.

United's confidence was shattered but the board stood by their manager, even though there were calls in the Press and from United supporters who had seen enough. Following the Maine Road thrashing and an early season run of six defeats and two draws in eight games, a banner declaring "Three years of excuses and it's still crap... Ta-ra Fergie" was unfurled at Old Trafford. He would later describe the period as his "darkest time in football".

The Old Trafford derby in early February saw the Reds just two points outside the relegation zone. Mel Machin's reward for the 5-1 win was the sack two months later, with chairman Peter Swales claiming his former manager's lack of personality and affinity with the supporters was ultimately his downfall. With Joe Royle electing to remain as Oldham manager following a City approach, former Everton boss Howard Kendall accepted the role and quickly brought in experienced campaigners like Peter Reid, Alan Harper, Wayne Clarke and Mark Ward as he prepared a "dogs of war" approach to the battle ahead. It would pay-off, too, and he went into his first derby with a fine record of just one defeat in six games plus a mean defensive record of three goals conceded during that run. Both teams desperately needed the points, but they would be shared as Clayton Blackmore's second-half header was rubbed out by a 30-yard equalizer from the unlikely boot of Ian Brightwell five minutes later to earn City a 1-1 draw.

Rumours that a last-minute penalty from Brian McClair had saved Ferguson's job may or may not have been true, but that equalizer at Nottingham Forest kept United in the FA Cup and, four months later, they had won the trophy against Crystal Palace. The pressure was off Ferguson, for the time being, and United also managed to finish in 13th, a place higher than City who were on the same points but had an inferior goal difference. FA Cup or not, the Blues had justifiably earned the bragging rights for the first time in a number of years and deservedly enjoyed their summer more than they had for almost a decade.

Days from the Sack, then Fergie Delivers

1989–1996

"Alex Ferguson believed he'd identified the final piece of his jigsaw when he brought the erratic, but gifted, French striker Eric Cantona to Old Trafford."

United returned to the scene of the 1989 derby massacre with understandable trepidation. They weren't used to having their noses rubbed in the dirt, and though the draw at Old Trafford a few months earlier had restored some pride, another defeat would be hard to take.

City had continued to strengthen their squad, with Tony Coton, Niall Quinn and Neil Pointon added, while Alex Ferguson had brought in Neil Webb from Nottingham Forest and Denis Irwin from Oldham Athletic.

The Blues had started the season strongly, with just one defeat in nine games suggesting Howard Kendall had already found the right blend and balance, while United had lost four and won four of their opening fixtures. Just two places separated the teams in the table with City in fifth and the Reds seventh.

The 113th league derby would also become one of the most exciting, though United feared another thrashing when they went 2-0 down after just 27 minutes thanks to two classy finishes from David

White. The next goal would prove vital for both teams and, on 37 minutes, Mark Hughes' header beat Coton to make it 2-1 – the Reds were back in the game. White saw a header crash back off the bar as he was denied his hat-trick midway through the second half and City looked in control of proceedings but, crucially, didn't add to their lead until the 79th minute when defender Colin Hendry burst forward, played a one-two with Quinn and then tucked the ball past Les Sealey for what was surely the winner. As the Kippax celebrated United boss Ferguson could have been forgiven for feeling déjà vu and dread in equal measure. He needed something extraordinary from his players and Brian McClair provided exactly that, scoring twice in the space of three minutes to send the travelling fans wild. First he dispossessed sub Ian Brightwell and then raced forward to drill a low shot past Coton, and then he headed home a Webb corner with a powerful header moments later. Gary Pallister's late volley very nearly won the game for the Reds. Within a few weeks Howard Kendall resigned to start a second spell at Everton, shocking the football world and leaving the untried Peter Reid to take control.

United used the derby as a springboard for an impressive campaign and they beat City 1-0 in the return fixture at the start of May thanks to a 17-year-old Ryan Giggs scoring the only goal on his debut. That wasn't enough to catch the Blues who would finish above their neighbours in the league for the first time in 13 years.

Ferguson again brought silverware back to Old Trafford a few days later, however, to head off any criticism that might have been coming his way. Having already reached the League Cup final, and finished runners-up to Sheffield Wednesday, United claimed their first major European trophy for 23 years by beating Barcelona 2-1 to lift the European Cup Winners' Cup in Rotterdam.

The 1991/92 meetings were unspectacular and very even, the first at Maine Road ending 0-0 and the return finishing 1-1 with Giggs opening the scoring and Keith Curle levelling from the spot for

10-man City in the latter. The Reds somehow lost the title, losing three of their last four games to finish second in the table behind Leeds United, stretching their wait to win the league to 25 years. City finished fifth for a second successive year and seemed to have established themselves as a top-six side, but the Blues craved success and 16 years had passed since a City captain last lifted a trophy. United did end their League Cup hoodoo beating Nottingham Forest 2-1 at Wembley, further compounding the Blues' silverware drought.

If the Reds had been missing anything it was a touch of genius and arrogance – something not witnessed since George Best left the club. Alex Ferguson believed he'd identified the final piece of his jigsaw when he brought the erratic, but gifted, French striker Eric Cantona to Old Trafford. It was to prove inspired as the 1992/93 season finally saw United end their long wait for a league title. The lowest Old Trafford derby crowd in memory – 35,408 – witnessed a 2-1 win for United in December thanks to goals from Paul Ince and Mark Hughes; Niall Quinn bagged City's consolation. With United locked in a three-way battle for pole position along with Norwich and Aston Villa, the second meeting had even more riding on it than usual.

As ever, the neighbourly "love" ensured the Blues were determined to put a spanner in the works for United, and a 1-1 draw hardly enhanced the Reds' challenge. Quinn was again the mark for City, with Cantona bagging his first goal against the Blues, and United hit peak form at exactly the right time shortly after, winning their final seven games to secure the first Premier League title. A crushing 5-2 last-day defeat to Everton robbed the Blues of a third successive fifth-place finish and they instead ended in ninth in what would be Peter Reid's last full season in charge.

Reid would resign four games into the 1993/94 season, with United's success making the Maine Road hot seat an uncomfortable place to be. Some City fans felt Reid's tactics were too direct and a poor start to the new campaign resulted in the board demanding his No.2 Sam Ellis be replaced. Reid stood by his man and his position became untenable. Brian Horton was his shock replacement as City entered a time of great instability; this was further compounded by the fact the Reds were now dominating English football. In fact, they were league leaders going into the 119th league meeting and, even with just 13 games played, were already 20 points clear of Horton's men.

The first meeting was particularly dramatic as Niall Quinn scored two goals in 10 first-half minutes to give his team a surprise 2-0 lead at the break. The Big Irishman had now scored for the third derby in a row, but this was to be a classic game of two halves and a painful one for City fans who hadn't suffered a home derby loss since 1985. Eric Cantona was the architect of the Blues' downfall, turning in a virtuoso performance in the second period and dragging United back into the contest on 52 minutes with a fierce shot that gave Tony Coton no chance. The same player then levelled the scores with just 10 minutes to go and, with all the momentum with the visitors, Roy Keane, signed from Nottingham Forest for a record £3.75m, slid home the winner with just three minutes remaining.

The chasm in Manchester football was widening all the time, with the Blues unable to compete in the transfer market and United adding Peter Schmeichel and Andrei Kanchelskis to the team. With relegation having looked a distinct possibility at one stage, before the next derby Horton had added Uwe Rosler, Paul Walsh and Peter Beagrie to his side in a bid to pep up a stale frontline, and the only game the Blues would lose in their last 10 games was the 2-0 defeat at Old Trafford – Cantona again on the mark twice. United went on to win the title again, while the Blues weren't mathematically safe until the final day of the season.

Such was the strength of United's squad there was a feeling of resignation in the blue half of Manchester that it could be a long time before City were once again challenging their neighbours for trophies.

But if the 1993/94 derbies had proved disappointing for the Blues, the 1994/95 clashes were unbearable. Both Manchester clubs were in the top 10, but not troubling the leaders, when they ran out at Old Trafford. City fans had been fearing a heavy defeat for a number of years, given the difference in squad quality and apparent growing gap between the clubs, and this was to be the day they had dreaded, as a rampant United swept the Blues aside.

While United had become progressively stronger City had gradually become weaker and things had finally come to a head. The scourge of the Blues, Eric Cantona, made it six goals in five derbies by opening the scoring after 24 minutes, but it then became the Andrei Kanchelskis show with the Russian winger bagging a first derby hat-trick since Francis Lee in 1970. Mark Hughes also scored as United ran out 5-0 winners with City well and truly beaten on the day. The memory of the Maine Road thrashing was finally banished in a merciless display by Ferguson's side.

The return derby came around all too quickly for City the following February and a bad-tempered 3-0 win put United back on top of the Premier League – just 26,368 watched the game as interest in the derby slipped to an all-time low and many wondered whether this showpiece match would ever regain its standing among Mancunians. Certainly Alex Ferguson would play his part in dumbing down the game in future years, but if the derby, now just over 100 years old, were to lose its attraction and interest, part of Manchester's sporting history would die with it. These were worrying times and there was no immediate end in sight.

It was little consolation for City fans that the Reds failed to win any trophies and finished second to Blackburn Rovers in the Premier League after failing to get the three points needed to leapfrog Blackburn on the final day during a 1-1 draw with West Ham. The Blues, for their part, had narrowly escaped relegation again and

Brian Horton was sacked as manager after a final day 3-2 home loss to QPR.

City fans demanded a big name with funds to rebuild a great team again and, with former hero Francis Lee now chairman after finally winning control of the club following a bitter boardroom takeover from Peter Swales, it appeared that might be possible. But there was to be no major investment, and the new manager – Alan Ball – distinctly underwhelmed the Blues' fans. Their fears were realized, too, when the former England World Cup winner made a disastrous start to his career at Maine Road, losing nine and drawing two of his first 11 games as boss. At least Lee brought in Georgian midfielder Georgi Kinkladze who quickly became the darling of the City faithful, but he was the one shining light in what was a very average side. The Blues lost 1-0 away to United during that dismal start under Ball, with Paul Scholes scoring the only goal of a forgettable game.

At least the City's form had improved by the time the teams met for an FA Cup fifth-round clash at Old Trafford. City had gathered 22 points from their previous 15 games and felt no real pressure as the clear underdogs in this game. It showed, too, as Kinkladze sent Rosler clear on 11 minutes and the German striker expertly lobbed Schmeichel to send the 10,000 travelling fans into dreamland, even if most of them feared the goal had come a little too early in the game! Then, controversy. Referee Alan Wilkie was the official who had sent Eric Cantona off at Crystal Palace after the Frenchman's Kung Fu kick at a Palace fan as he walked to the dressing room, resulting in a lengthy ban for the sulky striker.

Perhaps feeling partly responsible for denying the Reds their talisman, it seemed Wilkie couldn't wait to win the United fans over and, when Michael Frontzeck was deemed to have fouled the Frenchman from a corner, the official awarded a penalty. It was a harsh decision, no matter which team you followed, but Cantona didn't complain and planted the ball past Eike Immel to level the scores, much to the chagrin of all connected with City who knew it was hard enough to win at Old Trafford without the referee seemingly biased. To City's credit it looked as though they might hang on for a replay, but there was further heartache to come when Lee Sharpe converted Ryan Giggs' cross 10 minutes from time to confirm United's passage into the last eight.

There was still one more derby to be played out during the 1995/96 campaign and, thankfully, it was a thrilling affair packed with drama and incident. City needed something from the game as they continued to fight relegation, while the Reds were surging towards a third title in four years. The game went to form early on, Cantona scoring from the spot to give the visitors the lead, but the Blues then hit back when Mikhail Kavelashvili – a Georgian compatriot of Kinkladze and recent arrival – equalized, but Andy Cole restored United's lead before the break.

City refused to give in and when Rosler slammed home a cracking effort to make it 2-2, the Blues' fans even dared to dream of a victory but, it wasn't to be, as Ryan Giggs smashed home a spectacular winner just 60 second later.

Imagine being a City fan in Manchester over the next few weeks as they watched their team relegated on the final day of the season, their rivals crowned Premier League champions and, just to rub salt in, collect the FA Cup too, with a 1-0 win over Liverpool to complete the coveted "double".

It would be four long years before City would return to the top flight, by which time the Manchester derby had taken on a completely new identity.

We'll Meet Again...

1996–2002

"With United, we'd all grown up together; we all wanted to win the biggest trophy in football. We did it together."

David Beckham

As City slipped through the divisions, United slipped through the gears and the gap between the two clubs was never greater. During the four years, between the Blues' relegation and return to the top flight, the Reds went from strength to strength, while their neighbours struggled with life in what is today the Championship, eventually slipping into the third tier for the first time.

City managers came and went and each seemed intent on doing worse than their predecessor in a dizzying time for supporters and the playing staff. Asa Hartford filled in following Alan Ball's dismissal, a little over 12 months after he'd arrived, but was then replaced by former Manchester United favourite, Steve Coppell, a man who had been a thorn in the Blues' side during the late 1970s and early 1980s. He was the first former United player to manage City, yet he was afforded a warm welcome by the fans, still relieved Ball had gone. But Coppell would only compound the situation by quitting his position after only six games and 33 days in charge. His reign at the club is the shortest of any City manager to date.

After Coppell came Phil Neal, a man who had become known as Graham Taylor's "yes man" in an infamous documentary on the former England manager. A fish out of water, he was gone in the blink of an eye, but not before irreparable damage had been done with seven defeats in 10 games.

The City fans were then yet again underwhelmed by the appointment of former Nottingham Forest boss Frank Clark who was as dour off the field as the tactics he employed on it. Eventually, after 14 months in charge, he was dismissed and former City striker Joe Royle was given the task of saving a sinking ship.

The Blues changed managers and playing personnel at a dizzying rate before Joe Royle finally guided City back to the Premier League following back-to-back promotions in 1998/99 and 1999/2000.

During that time United added two Premier League titles, the FA Cup, and a dramatic 2-1 win over Bayern Munich secured the Champions League and an unprecedented treble. City would choose the lowest point in their history to coincide with the most successful United side ever! Such is the lot of a Blue – at least during the Reds' period of dominance.

The 2000/01 campaign finally saw the resumption of the fixture all of Manchester took notice of, although the fixture was no longer the event of the season.

City were rebuilding, gradually, but United had a golden generation of youth players who had progressed through to the senior squad including Giggs, Scholes, Phil and Gary Neville, and David Beckham, all of whom had formed the backbone of the treble-winning team – and the side that had won titles in 2000.

City's enjoyment at the resumption of the derby lasted all of 90 seconds. The first meeting in November was settled by a Beckham goal with less than two minutes on the clock.

In the months between the teams meeting again in April, City had slipped to second bottom, while the Reds would win the league comfortably. City drew the game 1-1 but the result made little difference to either side and, for the fourth time in five years, City changed divisions and would play their football in the second tier of English football during the 2001/02 season – and they would do it under the tutelage of Kevin Keegan who had replaced Joe Royle, controversially sacked at the end of the campaign.

Keegan breezed into Maine Road with typical enthusiasm and energy and wasted no time in fashioning an attack-minded team in his own image for the new season. In came Eyal Berkovic and Ali Benarbia, with Stuart Pearce brought in to shore up the back four. With Shaun Goater finding the net on a regular basis the Blues soon pulled away from the chasing pack to comfortably win the Division One title and return to the Premier League at the first attempt.

Meanwhile, United had a rare campaign when they failed to win anything, finishing third in the table. So the scene was set for the 2002/03 season and a very special Manchester derby in Moss Side.

The date of 9th November 2002 will forever be etched into the minds of the City fans who were at the last ever Maine Road derby, which was always going to be an emotional day for the supporters and players.

City had been planning to move away from their home of 80 years for some time and, when the opportunity came to take residence in the 2002 Commonwealth Games City of Manchester Stadium, plans were drawn up to turn the athletics venue into a 48,000-capacity football stadium once the Games ended.

With the Blues pumped up and ready to give their home of 80 years a proper send off the home support hoped their team wouldn't let the occasion get the better of them. City fans will tell you their team usually do exactly the opposite of what they want them to but that wouldn't happen this time – this was one of those rare days when everything went according to plan and it all made for a day nobody in blue would ever forget.

There was only one option – City had to win their last Manchester derby at Maine Road. Kevin Keegan underlined how important this game was and how it would be talked about for many years to come. If they lost, people would wonder how it was possible. If they won, they would be heroes who stepped up to the plate when it was needed the most.

The City fans were ready and the ground was a cauldron of noise and passion – the question was, were the players ready? The answer would be revealed in the 90 minutes that followed the referee's whistle to begin the game.

United gifted City an opening goal after just four minutes, briefly played well enough to get back on terms quickly, but showed surprisingly little stomach for a fight once they went behind again to a bizarre Shaun Goater goal.

Never had Roy Keane's absence been so keenly felt. Without him City midfielders such as Eyal Berkovic and Danny Tiatto were allowed to run the game.

With David Beckham suspended United appeared leaderless and ineffective, and although Juan Veron initially looked capable of taking a hold in midfield, he faded so badly he was withdrawn in the second half.

Gary Neville, captain for the day, was responsible for allowing Goater to score one of the comedy goals of the season. The City fans even chanted, "There's only one Gary Neville" at one point, yet there was more amiss in this listless performance than a couple of defensive howlers. Despite deploying a five-man midfield with Ruud van Nistelrooy foraging alone up front, United lost that crucial battle to their City counterparts and could not even pick up the dangerous Berkovic when it was obvious his timing and distribution could hurt them.

That an upset was on the cards was clear from the manner in which City gained the upper hand as United's defence collectively self-destructed. Phil Neville's poor pass put Rio Ferdinand under pressure, the centre-half was unable to hold Anelka off and, though Goater's eventual shot was tame, Fabien Barthez inexplicably failed to hold it and succeeded only in presenting Anelka with an unmissable opportunity from three yards out.

City soon surrendered that lead when their own defence fell asleep four minutes later, Lucien Mettomo, in particular, allowing Ryan Giggs' cross to float past him and receive predictably deadly treatment from Ole Gunnar Solskjaer. The Blues went quiet for 20 minutes after that, as if anticipating the inevitable onslaught, but it never came. Then, just before the half-hour, Marc Vivien Foe attempted a cross-field pass to Niclas Jensen but sliced it so badly he almost hit a corner flag. The Cameroon midfielder was trudging back towards his own goal, hand raised in apology, when Gary Neville's attempt to shepherd the ball out for a goal kick went horribly wrong. Realizing the ball would not roll dead in time Neville tried to turn it back to Barthez and found only Goater, whose endeavour in chasing an apparently lost cause was fully rewarded when he effortlessly beat the goalkeeper from a narrow angle.

It was a sweet moment for the Blues' fans and for Goater; it was a triumph over adversity.

The return of the defensive jitters appeared to knock the stuffing out of United, who should have gone 3-1 down before the interval, when Anelka shot straight at Barthez after Goater had given him enough time to walk the ball round him.

Berkovic performed a similar favour at the start of the second half and this time Anelka ran into Barthez and unsuccessfully appealed for a penalty. The impressive Goater showed him how to do it two minutes later, again from Berkovic's prompting, when he calmly waited for Barthez to commit himself before lifting the ball over the Frenchman for his 100th City goal. "You couldn't get two more different strikers, but they are both quality players and their decision making was excellent," Keegan said later.

Peter Schmeichel was required to make late saves from Giggs and Solskjaer as City did their best to set up a nervous ending, though both attempts lacked conviction.

As far as City were concerned they were back and, with Kevin Keegan leading the charge, anything seemed possible.

City Plod On, Reds Charge Ahead

2002–2004

"Ali Benarbia said we hadn't given him Shaun long enough – and on the evidence of that he was probably right."

Kevin Keegan

City would confirm bragging rights for season 2002/03 in the Old Trafford return, which could have ended much better than it did but for an over fussy referee saving United's blushes late on. Sir Alex Ferguson was furious. As if watching his players hoist a white flag at Maine Road last November was not galling enough, he was left to assess the damage from another morale-sapping afternoon and wish he could shut himself away in a darkened room until the events he'd witnessed had been long forgotten.

Meanwhile, City were left indebted to a player who, 15 years before, was summoned to Ferguson's office and informed he wasn't good enough for a career at Old Trafford. Ferguson may have been right about Shaun Goater, then 17, but the one-time Manchester United apprentice had never been short of self-belief and, with three goals against his former employers in two games during the current season, he had proved a point to the man who let him go, if nothing else.

The header with which he turned this meeting of Mancunian minds upside-down came four minutes from the end of what, at one point, had looked like just another routine United victory. Nobody could dispute that Goater had an impeccable sense of timing, but it was particularly evident here considering he had replaced Robbie Fowler only nine seconds earlier, thus scoring the quickest goal by a substitute in Premier League history.

City would leave Old Trafford feeling aggrieved not to have completed a first league double over United since the 1969/70 season. In the third and final minute of stoppage-time Goater turned the ball beyond Roy Carroll again. This time, though, Nicolas Anelka was penalized for allowing an awkwardly bouncing ball to flick off his right glove, however unintentional it was, after Marc-Vivien Foé's cross had deflected off Mikaël Silvestre's instep and spun on to the crossbar. Anelka did not complain vociferously but that did not dilute the feeling that, just then, United's luck was in.

Ruud van Nistelrooy had turned in the low, teasing cross from Ryan Giggs that invited his 27th goal of the season to put the Reds ahead, but the Dutch striker had, thereafter, missed a host of chances to put the game beyond all reasonable doubt.

"We had so many chances that it's a game we should have won," said Ferguson. "When you spurn that many opportunities it can cost you."

There were certainly signs of Keegan's players being encouraged by the Reds' inability to kill the game off, even if there was a conspicuous lack of momentum about their forward thrusts, and few indications of a blossoming relationship between Fowler and Anelka.

Keegan also had to contend with Peter Schmeichel dropping out 20 minutes before the kick-off, his calf injury denying him a return to the arena where he spent eight trophy-lade years, thrusting Carlo Nash into an unexpected starting role.

Yet, once they shook their heads clear, there was an admirable quality about the manner in which City, and the magical Eyal Berkovic in particular, persevered at their task.

"We have to be delighted," said Keegan. "We've played

Manchester United twice now and we're unbeaten. I don't know how many sides will be able to say that at the end of the season, but I would guess you could count them on one hand, or even two fingers."

The Blues had taken four points off the Reds – something only Bolton Wanderers could claim to have done that season – and though United went on to win the title again, City had every right to be pleased with a solid return to the top flight.

The 2003/04 season would again see City struggle to end their Old Trafford hoodoo which now stretched back 29 years. It was becoming a source of embarrassment for the Blues' fans that now travelled more in hope rather than expectation. It had to end sometime, of course, but it wouldn't be during this campaign, when Keegan's side surprisingly flirted with relegation having failed to build on a solid first season back in the top flight.

There were also rumblings across the city at Old Trafford too. United were in the process of a protracted takeover that would eventually see US businessman Malcolm Glazer buyout the Reds' shareholders at a cost close to $1.5 billion. Immediately, United would go from one of the most profitable clubs in the world to one that was heavily saddled with the new owners' previous debts – approximately $850m – due to the complicated nature over the deal. Though fiercely protested by supporters, there was actually very little they could do. Still, on the pitch, the Reds had plenty to smile about.

With United's new scoring sensation Cristiano Ronaldo forging a lethal partnership with the prolific Ruud van Nistelrooy the Reds were expected to defend their title and possibly pick up another trophy along the way. The first of two games in eight weeks between the teams took place in mid-December, with Paul Scholes and Van Nistelrooy giving United a 2-0 half-time lead. Shaun Wright-Phillips pulled City back into contention after 52 minutes but Scholes added a third on 73 minutes to seal the points, and a 3-1 win, putting United top of the table and leaving the Blues in 12th.

City fans wondered if the FA Cup might end their long wait for silverware, especially after Keegan's side overturned a 3-0 half-time deficit at White Hart Lane to stage a remarkable second-half come back to win 4-3 – and that with only 10 men following Joey Barton's dismissal at the break.

The "reward" was a trip to face United, who had surprisingly lost 3-2 at home to Middlesbrough the week before in the league. Backed by some 10,000 fans the Blues went into the game with high hopes and when, at half-time, Kevin Keegan informed his players that they'd been presented with "the best opportunity you'll ever get at this ground" the Blues players maybe should have taken more notice.

Keegan's team created plenty of chances, but wasted most of them and, given the numerical advantage they had after Gary Neville's dismissal, it was a sloppy 90 minutes from a team who weren't good enough to be wasteful in front of goal.

City had no apparent game plan so, when Scholes, Van Nistelrooy and Ronaldo gave United a 3-0 lead, it wasn't entirely unexpected. Indeed, the Reds were all but out of sight by the time Michael Tarnat crashed a shot into the roof of the net to give the travelling army a glimmer of hope and, even then, Van Nistelrooy popped up at the other end to restore United's three-goal lead shortly after.

There was still time for Fowler to catch out Tim Howard with a quickly taken free-kick, though it scarcely mattered given that there were a couple of minutes left to play. Too little, too late.

"They scored from half-chances and we missed gilt-edged chances," said Keegan, whose position was looking more fragile with each passing game. At the after match Press conference he informed reporters he would see them next week. With an ailing team and a sense that he could no longer motivate his team or, perhaps, himself, it seemed a matter of time before he called it a day at City.

Meanwhile, the Reds would go all the way to the final where they won the FA Cup at a canter, beating Championship side Millwall 3-0 at Wembley.

Following on from the previous season's farewell derby at Maine Road would be a tough act to follow but the inaugural derby at the City of Manchester Stadium did not disappoint. Just a few weeks after being knocked out of the cup the Blues turned in their best performance of the season against a stunned and well-beaten United.

This match was to be a happy occasion for City fans as they saw United's title hopes disintegrate at Eastlands while winning their first home game in nearly five months.

The Reds came into the game having won just once in their previous five games, while City were holding their own and looking for a morale-boosting win over their neighbours in what would turn out to be an entertaining end-to-end encounter between the Manchester giants.

City started brightly and were ahead after just three minutes when Fowler scored from close range before celebrating in the same manner Porto boss José Mourinho had when his team knocked United out of the Champions League – in front of the Reds' fans, of course.

Ronaldo could have equalized immediately but saw his shot hit the post after David James had kept out Paul Scholes' effort and, perhaps, the tilt of the game, in that moment, was decided.

Half an hour later the lead was doubled as a Claudio Reyna effort deflected from the midriff of Scholes for Jonathan Macken to send the ball skipping beyond Howard. The forward was on United's books as a youngster and £1m of the £5m that City paid Preston for him is thought to have been forwarded to Old Trafford, but that compensation cannot have been any comfort here.

When Paul Scholes reduced the deficit to 2-1 in the 35th minute from a Ryan Giggs pass expectations were that United would soon find their way to level terms. But the luck was to be with City on this

ABOVE: The victorious Manchester United team return home following their 1-0 victory over Bristol City in the 1909 FA Cup final at Wembley Stadium. City had won the trophy five years earlier.

LEFT: Billy Meredith, still with Manchester United but torn between both Manchester clubs during a glorious career that began and ended with City, 1909.

1947: A record derby day crowd of 78,000 welcomes back the fixture all Manchester had waited for following the end of the Second World War – the game ended 0-0.

1947: The skippers meet ahead of the 45th Manchester derby at Maine Road.

1955: Tommy Taylor fires in a header that Dave Ewing blocks, while City captain Roy Paul watches on. City would go on to win 2-0 and progress through to the fifth round of the FA Cup.

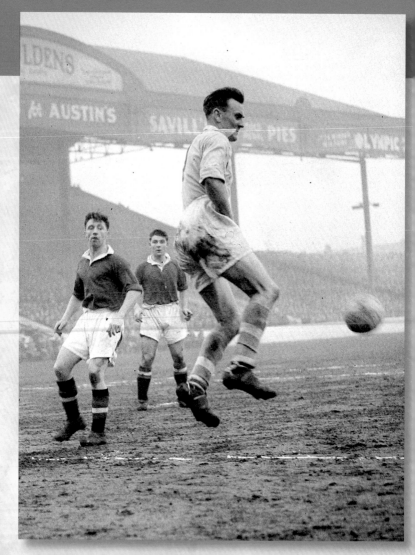

1955: Don Revie, the City forward who caused United so many problems during the Fifties as the integral part of "the Revie Plan".

ABOVE: The wreck of United's plane on the runway at Munich that killed so many of Matt Busby's brilliant young side, as well as City legend Frank Swift. A tragic day for Manchester and the world of football, 1958.

BELOW: United's Bobby Charlton scores his second goal of the game, watched by team-mates Denis Law and George Best, during a 2-1 win over City at Maine Road, 1967.

1968: Did fate have a hand in City's 1968 title win? The first attempt at the Old Trafford derby was postponed due to an icy pitch – the Blues won the re-arranged game 3-1.

1968: Derby day crowd trouble was becoming more and more common during the Sixties.

ABOVE: Alex Stepney picks the ball out of his net after being beaten by Colin Bell. City went on to record a crucial 3-1 win at Old Trafford on their way to the title in 1968.

BELOW: Francis Lee celebrates City's fourth and final goals at Newcastle to all but confirm the title, while United lost 2-0 at home to Sunderland to finish second, 1968.

ABOVE: United finally realize Sir Matt Busby's dream by winning the European Cup for the first time after a 4-1 win over Benfica in 1968.

BELOW: Bobby Charlton equalizes for United in the League Cup semi-final first leg at Maine Road, though the Blues would go on to win 2-1, 1969.

ABOVE: The men behind making Manchester the capital of world football – Joe Mercer and Sir Matt Busby at the peak of their powers, 1969.

BELOW: Colin Bell, the scourge of United, scores his second in the 4-0 league win over the Reds at Maine Road, 1969.

ABOVE: Mike Doyle – happy to wind up the United fans before the derby to the extent he received death threats, 1970.

LEFT: George Best and Denis Law – two of the main reasons United were so successful in the late 1960s, pictured in 1971.

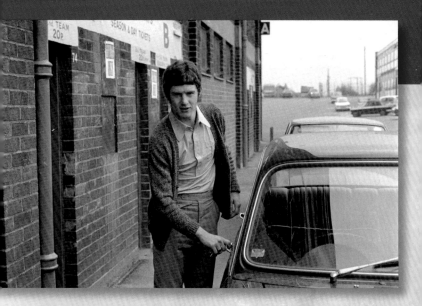

ABOVE: Brian Kidd towards the end of his United career. The boyhood Blue would join City in 1976 and almost match his total with United during three successful seasons at Maine Road, 1972.

BELOW: Denis Law is disconsolate after condemning United to Division Two with a late winner at Old Trafford, 1974.

ABOVE: Police keep United fans away from the dressing rooms after their relegation had been confirmed with a 1-0 home defeat to City, 1974.

BELOW: Steve Coppell – the United winger who would go on to briefly manage City, 1979.

ABOVE: Alex Ferguson (pictured here in 1986) says hello to the Stretford End – few could have imagined the success the new United boss would go on to enjoy – though it wasn't without its early hiccups…

BELOW: Ian Bishop scores City's third as the Blues go on to win 5-1 at Maine Road, 1989.

ABOVE: A United fan pleads with the board to stick with Alex Ferguson as rumours he may be fired circulate prior to an FA Cup tie at Nottingham Forest, 1990.

BELOW: Ryan Giggs scores his first goal for United after the ball takes a deflection off Colin Hendry. United won 1-0, 1991.

ABOVE: Eric Cantona makes his first derby appearance in a 2-1 win over City at Old Trafford in 1992.

BELOW: Future City boss Mark Hughes scores the winner against the Blues at Old Trafford, 1992.

ABOVE: Francis Lee (pictured here in 1994) returns as chairman of Manchester City. Despite the initial delight, Lee's reign wouldn't be successful.

BELOW: The new power in Manchester? Roberto Mancini and skipper Vincent Kompany present the Premier League trophy to thousands of ecstatic supporters as the Blues win the title for the first time in 44 years, 2012.

occasion – proved beyond all doubt when Ronaldo crashed a shot against the bar with 37 minutes on the clock.

Ferguson's side, nonetheless, appeared to have the remedy to their own problems. There could have been a blitz of goals prior to the interval, had Ronaldo been luckier and Giggs more accurate in their finishing. Progress was far more difficult to achieve thereafter, but it took another mistake to polish off United.

Silvestre's touch was poor as he attempted to control a through-ball from Paul Bosvelt and it slithered off his foot. Trevor Sinclair was predatory, bustling in behind the Frenchman to clip a shot home in the 73rd minute. United were doomed to one of their most dispiriting experiences.

United were bedevilled by defensive mistakes so, by the 90th minute when Shaun Wright-Phillips kept the ball in play as it rolled along the paint of the right touchline, moved inside and, with Wes Brown barring his path, directed an angled chip over the head of the goalkeeper Tim Howard and in off the crossbar, it wasn't entirely unexpected and, as the City fans went crazy, the Reds cursed their first visit to the City of Manchester Stadium as much as they had their final visit to Maine Road.

The three points also pulled Keegan's side away from the drop zone, while United's main concern was finishing 15 points behind eventual champions Arsenal – nicknamed "the Invincibles" after completing their league programme without losing a single game. The Reds finished third in the table, but City's 16th-place berth suggested the "Keegan Factor" had almost run its course...

Psycho Takes On Fergie

2004–2006

"'This team has bounced back before. I'm not worried about them bouncing back again."

Alex Ferguson

With the vast sums of Sky TV money now sloshing around the Premier League the Blues could ill afford another stint outside the top flight. The odd derby win was obviously nice for City fans but they wondered if they would ever compete with their neighbours again on a level playing field. The 1980s had seen the gap begin to widen, and the Blues' mid-1990s relegation, mismanagement at all levels and slip to the third tier now looked to have caused irreparable damage.

It was an awful prospect that only the occasional 90 minutes here and there might be City's lot unless there was some drastic change of direction. City midfielder Joey Barton summed up the fans' frustrations. The controversial Academy product was succinct in his view of the future of the club when he said: "You have to face facts. We have not brought quality in. One or two have done all right but not enough to take the team onto the next level. We can't gamble on players who have scored six goals in six games in a league in Belgium. I know a lot of the supporters who don't know whether to buy their season tickets. They go out and work hard. It is a lot of money to buy a season ticket here, and they are not getting value for money."

Going into the 2004/05 season little had changed and City were reliant on the personal fortune of owner John Wardle who had taken over from Franny Lee – whereas United, commercially, were light years ahead. Blues' fans (and most of football) cast envious glances over to Chelsea where billionaire owner Roman Abramovich was pumping millions of pounds into team strengthening. Why, they wondered, does nobody invest in us? It was a valid question that, at that time, had no logical answer.

Pre-season saw Wayne Rooney arrive at Old Trafford to bolster an already impressive frontline of Giggs, Ronaldo and Van Nistelrooy. By contrast City had Fowler, Macken and Antoine Sibierski. It looked set to be another long season over at the City of Manchester Stadium – and that's exactly what it proved to be.

United challenged on all fronts but it was to be megabucks Chelsea's season in the Premier League. The Manchester derbies were dour, unattractive affairs with the Keegan brand of football sadly lacking.

The first meeting ended 0-0 at Old Trafford, with United reduced to 10 men following Alan Smith's dismissal.

"With that sort of form we're not good enough in terms of the championship," Ferguson opined afterwards. "It's not championship form and I can't excuse anyone at the club for that. Nine parts of our game is good but the tenth part, the most important one, is just not there. It's not good enough."

Ferguson was entitled to reflect on the statistics and to wonder how the Manchester derby had not finished with one of its more emphatic scorelines. United were calculated as having 82% of possession at one stage, and 67% in total, with only 7% of the game played in the third of the pitch directly in front of Roy Carroll.

Kevin Keegan had half a dozen players missing and felt no need to apologize as he reflected upon their total of precisely zero shots on target throughout the entire match.

Instead, this was a day when Keegan's defenders excelled and the likes of Shaun Wright-Phillips and Nicolas Anelka had to make do with bit-part contributions. Lesser players might have crumbled under the pressure but Danny Mills, Richard Dunne and Sylvain Distin defended stoutly with brave interceptions and the countless times they headed the ball away from beneath their own crossbar.

Stephen Jordan, a product of the Blues' Academy, had a day to remember. His goal-line clearance to deny Louis Saha a fourth-minute goal was the outstanding moment of the match, although it was not the only time that David James was indebted to one of his colleagues: the goalkeeper even gave Steve McManaman a kiss on the forehead after he had turned Smith's overhead kick off the line.

The return saw a more interesting contest for the neutral, with at least a couple of goals.

Wayne Rooney's battle with Richard Dunne proved to be the key in this battle, with the striker just edging the honours.

Dunne, the City skipper, was having the best of it for two thirds of the game, but the problem with Rooney is that you can't afford to switch off for a second or the England striker is sure to punish you. In what would turn out to be Keegan's last Manchester derby as City boss, Rooney would be involved in both goals to varying degrees.

With the game seemingly headed for a 0-0 draw Roy Keane released Gary Neville, and the full-back's low cross was fired to the edge of the six-yard box where Rooney's desire and anticipation had got him to the ball first at the near post. His finish then deflected off Dunne to find the net. It had been a long wait for that decisive moment. The match tried the patience of the crowd and tested the perseverance of a United team that had been in difficulties during the first half.

Chelsea were nine points clear of the Reds in the Premier League but instinct demanded United did not give up the fight while there was still a mathematical chance of turning things around.

City's wastefulness during the game's early exchanges eventually came back to haunt them. Kiki Musampa and Steve McManaman should have. Having sold Nicolas Anelka at the very end of the transfer window they lacked a cutting edge in front of goal and Fowler had neither the pace nor presence to punish United. Then, with 15 minutes remaining, Neville picked out Rooney from his throw-in and the forward sent in a dangerous cross. David James failed to make his intentions known for Dunne did not seem to believe that his goalkeeper was about to collect the ball. The Irishman sought to clear but merely bent the ball into the far corner of his own net – not a new experience for Dunne who had a history of own goals during his time with City – and from there on, it was game over.

Keegan saw the writing on the wall and, unable to motivate either himself or the team to the levels he demanded, he quit his post after a limp 1-0 home defeat to Bolton, leaving his No.2 Stuart Pearce to take over in a temporary role until the end of the season.

Pearce immediately galvanized his ailing troops and City's late charge for a UEFA Cup spot won the man they once called "Psycho" a two-year contract.

The Reds reached the FA Cup final but lost to Arsenal and failed on all other fronts, too, in a disappointing season by their recent standards. The thing with the reds, however, was that it was inevitable they wouldn't go too long without winning something – it was in their DNA.

Pearce was showing some promise as manager and, by the time the Blues went to Old Trafford in September, his team hadn't tasted defeat since March. City continued a trend of bringing the odd former United or Liverpool legend to the club – the trouble was, they were always well past their peak and the signings didn't sit entirely well with the supporters. Ex-Reds' favourite Andy Cole, now nearing the end of a long, illustrious career, was signed to lead their line along with former Aston Villa striker Darius Vassell, forming a new-look attack, and City actually went into the derby in third, one place above United.

Asked to name United's traditional rivals he claimed, in order, Liverpool, Arsenal and Leeds were now the Reds' true rivals. "Manchester City are not a problem for me," he said, and the lack of passion showed in this derby perhaps underlined this sentiment had filtered through to his own players.

City showed more bite and desire and, though Van Nistelrooy scored the opener on 45 minutes, Joey Barton levelled after 75 to earn his team a well-earned point.

City held their own for a while and were in ninth by the time the teams resumed battle in January 2006. United were unbeaten in 12 league games, while Pearce's men were patchy and unpredictable.

United, by the standards they'd set themselves in recent years, were struggling. They came into this game against City knowing there was little or no chance they would close the 13-point gap on leaders Chelsea, and their indiscipline shone through during a wretched afternoon for Sir Alex Ferguson's men.

That they should choose one of their worst displays of the season for a meeting with the Blues was down to nothing else other than bad timing, though nobody doubted that, by the end of the game, City had thoroughly deserved the three points on offer.

There were many reasons for United leaving Eastlands with nothing: an embarrassing, curtailed debut of Patrice Evra, the dismissal of Cristiano Ronaldo and a terrible display by French full-back Mikaël Silvestre.

To City fans it seemed incredulous that United fans should criticize Sir Alex Ferguson, given his record at Old Trafford, but there it was, the Reds weren't going to win the title and, for some, the buck stopped firmly at the manager's door. Others demanded the most successful manager in English football history be replaced.

City were sharper, showed more passion and determination, and goals from Trevor Sinclair and Darius Vassell gave the hosts a 2-0 lead at the break, with Stephen Ireland and Andy Cole providing the assists. Things got better for the Blues, too, with Ronaldo's lunge at Andy Cole resulting in a red card from referee Steve Bennett after 65 minutes, much to the delight of the City fans who took no small amount of pleasure in waving the Portugal star down the tunnel. As Ronaldo walked off, still protesting, so too went United's chance of turning the game around.

"He didn't get a foul for a very bad tackle," said Ferguson, in Ronaldo's defence. "He got a bit frustrated with that. He's not that type of player and it was a bit rash more than vicious. He's not touched the player, he's not gone near him but the referee has decided it's a red card; maybe he should look at it again. Different referees have different interpretations and we had Steve Bennett."

Ruud van Nistelrooy eventually pulled one back, ensuring a nail-biting finale for the City fans, but Robbie Fowler took special delight in confirming the win when he made it 3-1 in injury time with a typically assured finish – his eighth career goal against the Reds and third for the Blues against the old enemy – to send the City of Manchester Stadium into dreamland.

"This team has bounced back before," said Ferguson, defiant to the last. "I'm not worried about them bouncing back again."

The Reds at least added the Carling Cup to their collection in February but, again, that was to be their only piece of silverware and the title again evaded them with another third-place finish. The Blues won four and lost 11 of their final 15 games and it seemed Pearce's tenure may come to a quick end, but with little money to spend there seemed little point in changing managers; however, 12 months further down the line and the board probably wished they had brought a fresh face in.

Reds Regenerate, City Turn to Sven

2006–2010

"If I'm asked a question I will give an honest answer. Did Corradi go down cheaply? Yes, he did. The referee got it right. Nineteen other managers in this league might give you some bullshit answer but I'm not one of them."

Stuart Pearce

For City fans the 2006/07 campaign was as painful as any relegation campaign. The Blues fans were used to excitement and living on the edge of their nerves, but the moribund fayre Stuart Pearce's side served up during this campaign was almost too much to bear, particularly with United having reinvigorated themselves yet again.

As City's supporters were continually reminded it had been 32 years since the Blues last beat United on their own ground, and the evidence from the next Mancunian derby suggested it would be another 32 years before that particular statistic was put to bed.

The truth was if visiting teams were to stand any chance at Old Trafford the secret was to quieten the crowd, nullify United's early threat and build from those solid foundations. Good advice for any team travelling to the Reds' fortress but not something the Blues took on board.

City's defending actually encouraged their hosts from the moment, six minutes in, that Sylvain Distin failed wretchedly to intercept Ronaldo's low cross and Wayne Rooney fired home from close range.

The 3,000 City fans then watched in disbelief as three different players made apologetic gestures after Louis Saha turned in Gabriel Heinze's cross right on half-time. City were proving their own worst enemies but, with Pearce's two-pronged attack consisting of ineffective duo Bernardo Corradi and Georgios Samaras, it was hardly surprising they were trailing 2-0 without so much as a whimper.

Where was the passion? Where was the drive and determination to fight for the shirt and to represent Manchester City and the supporters who had followed them to football hell and back? Not only was it not good enough, it wasn't acceptable. The team in blue did not entirely lack endeavour but there was a conspicuous deficiency in guile and it wasn't until the introduction of Stephen Ireland at half-time that things began to improve.

Ireland, easily the club's best passer and creative talent, was continually overlooked by Pearce and it is a mystery why this was so. The point was underlined when Ireland left Nemanja Vidic on his backside – no mean feat – and set up Hatem Trabelsi to make it 2-1 – affording hopes of a most unlikely point or better.

As the United backlash failed to materialize City ignored the host's surprising invitation to attack and Richard Dunne was badly at fault when Rooney crossed for Ronaldo to score the decisive third.

Then the flop signing that Corradi had been underlined his ineffectiveness to score by legal means with a penalty-seeking dive that earned him a second yellow card instead. Corradi's dismissal was embarrassing and ended all hope of the Blues taking anything from this game.

Pearce, for all his limitations as City manager, was as honest as the day was long. He was a hard figure to dislike even though his team was struggling after his initial, inspirational start to life as the Blues' boss.

"There's no point buttering it up," said Pearce. "If I'm asked a question I will give an honest answer. Did he (Corradi) go down cheaply? Yes, he did. The referee got it right. Nineteen other managers in this league might give you some bullshit answer but I'm not one of them. If I say he was scythed down, you're only going to think I'm an idiot when you see it on television. So I'll speak the truth. Any chance some of the other managers coming out and doing the same?"

One scenario City fans had always dreaded was either being relegated by United or, equally as bad, have them win the league at Maine Road or the City of Manchester Stadium. In 80 years that scenario never happened, but the Blues' new home was about to experience exactly that after just three years of residence.

It's fair to assume that Sir Alex Ferguson would rather have won the league at Old Trafford, but winning at City's home was a more than acceptable experience for the Reds, whose travelling fans perhaps relished the prospect even more than on their own turf.

To rub salt in the wounds of any city rival is an opportunity not to be passed up; it would be the same if Arsenal could win the league at Spurs, Liverpool clinch the league at Everton, and so on.

Stuart Pearce's City still had their reverse thrusters on and another season under the tenure of the former England legend would likely see the Blues lose their top-flight status, too.

The supporters wanted one thing – a successful side or, at the very least, one who gave their all and entertained where possible. A trophy every now and then surely wouldn't be too much to ask for either, would it?

The Blues' miserable record of just 10 home goals all season was the worst in the club's history and the worst of any top-flight club in 119 years of the Football League. It was unforgiveable and Pearce was, in managerial terms, a dead man walking and not without blame for the situation, either. Electing to splash virtually all his £6m transfer budget on the lightweight Georgios Samaras had been foolhardy to say the least

United accumulated more goals than all but one of Ferguson's eight previous title-winning sides but merely went through the paces on this occasion, knowing the Blues offered such little threat up front that one goal would be enough and that it would inevitably come along at some point. Observers, deprived of the true importance of this game, could have been forgiven, indeed, for wondering whether they had stumbled across a meaningless end-of-season friendly rather than a championship-deciding derby.

Cristiano Ronaldo's 34th-minute penalty settled the game and, when City were presented with a wonderful chance to take a point from the game, Darius Vassell's penalty was so poor it was half-expected – even by the player himself judging by his body language. This was a difficult day for any City fan but help was finally on the way. They just didn't know it at that moment in time.

The Reds also reached the FA Cup final but crashed out to AC Milan in the semis of the Champions League, while Blues' fans had suffered not seeing a home goal for seven successive Premier League home games. Things had to change, and they did.

Thailand Prime Minister Thaksin Shinawatra had been sniffing around the Premier League for some time, threatening to buy Liverpool at one point.

A controversial character who loved the limelight and the column inches his efforts afforded him in the English Press Shinawatra decided City were the perfect club to buy. He purchased the club and its debts for around £90m and immediately installed former England boss Sven-Goran Eriksson as manager. City fans, in general, weren't too interested in Shinawatra's background – he'd passed the FA's fit and proper test and was given the all clear to pump millions into the club. It was exactly what City fans had been waiting for and at least a path to bigger and better things was being cleared. Almost overnight everything changed: a rich owner and one of the game's most respected managers. Things would never be the same again; but what few realized at the time was that Shinawatra's raising of the club's profile was catching the imagination of somebody who had the financial means to blow the rest of world football out of the water – though that was still a little while off, yet. Eriksson wasted no time in bringing eight new players in at a cost of around £30m. It seemed there was a new signing every day for a week as Blues' fans scratched their heads at developments at their club. As ever, it was all or nothing with Manchester City FC.

City, at last, were making progress. The memory of a miserable season under Stuart Pearce was fading fast as the 2007/08 campaign started with a win at West Ham, a home victory (and goal) in the 1-0 win over Derby County and then the Manchester derby. Coming just three months after United had celebrated winning the title in the Blues' own backyard here was City's chance for revenge – and though City were outplayed for most of the game it was one they took gleefully.

"If you could have points for possession of the ball and for shots, on and off target, we would have lost," Sven-Goran Eriksson reflected at the end of a match in which not even the most impassioned City supporter would deny their team had been lucky. "But we scored a goal and they didn't."

"It will take a long time to explain," Sir Alex Ferguson acknowledged. "Especially when you consider the number of chances we have had, plus our possession in the final third of the pitch; we really should have made it count. We've just been wasteful in front of goal and that's the nuts and bolts of it. I don't think we can even say City were lucky."

The Blues had rode their luck as United laid siege to Kasper Schmeichel's goal and, in many ways, it was the most one-sided derby for years – but none of that mattered to the jubilant City fans who celebrated Geovanni's deflected first-half winner with the kind of unbridled joy so rarely seen at the City of Manchester Stadium in recent years.

The Blues' 1-0 win meant United had taken only two points from their first three games – their worst start for 15 years – and could be found languishing in 16th position on the Premier League table, while City were top having collected three wins from their first three games and a seven-point advantage over the Reds already. "We've got ourselves in an uphill fight now," said Ferguson. "Ten years ago we could have handled that because we have always been good in the second half of the season, and now we are going to have to be."

Though United had dominated, what Sven-Goran Eriksson's side lacked in quality they made up for in endeavour, from Dietmar Hamann and Michael Johnson in midfield to Richard Dunne and Micah Richards in defence. Richards, in particular, produced a colossal performance, making at least half a dozen telling interceptions or saving tackles, and proved what an immense talent he could be.

Things were definitely picking up in the blue half of the city but, as though spurred on, United were soon once again the team to beat.

The fixtures had produced an amazing coincidence this season too, with the 2007/08 Old Trafford derby falling four days after the 50th anniversary of the Munich air disaster. It was an occasion that demanded the utmost respect from both sets of fans.

The tension was palpable as the game began, but nobody need have worried. With United fans holding red and white scarves aloft the City fans followed suit and the moment was marked impeccably; Sir Alex even turning to applaud the away section for their behaviour. Both teams wore kits reminiscent of the 1957/58 season, but in a strange almost muted Old Trafford it was City who rose to the occasion.

It was the former Aston Villa striker who opened the scoring after a move from one end of the pitch to the other, via the debutant Benjani Mwaruwari, Petrov and Ireland, culminating in Vassell beating

Edwin van der Sar at the second attempt. The first had actually been going wide but Van der Sar was disorientated after saving at Ireland's feet. The entire United defence, in fact, seemed to have lost its bearings and it was the same again, on the verge of half-time, when Benjani glanced in Petrov's cross for his first goal since arriving from Portsmouth a few days earlier.

A United onslaught might have been anticipated throughout the second half but it failed to materialize and, ultimately, Carrick's late goal meant little on what was very much the Blues' day.

It was just the fillip the City fans had needed and it was a timely reminder to the Premier League that, if the Blues could get their act together and build on what had been a promising first season under Sven-Goran Eriksson, they could once again be a force to be reckoned with.

One or two more signings could see City really making an impression, yet with rumours Eriksson was facing the axe starting to surface, supporters started a "Save Our Sven" campaign. It was all in vain as the Blues ended the season with an astonishing 8-1 defeat at Middlesbrough to tarnish an otherwise solid 12 months' progress. Two days after the season finished Eriksson was indeed sacked and Blackburn Rovers boss Mark Hughes replaced him, leaving City fans wondering if their club had yet again shot itself in the foot.

United, unperturbed by the derby loss and driven on by the prolific Cristiano Ronaldo, surged on to an 18th top-flight title and also added a third Champions League trophy to their cabinet with a dramatic penalty shoot-out win over Chelsea in Moscow. So, in many ways, it was business as usual for both Manchester clubs, but the landscape and powerbase in the city was about to change.

Blue Moon Rising

2010–2011

"Mark Hughes must have cast an envious glance at the unsettled Tevez and wondered, 'what if…?' What if indeed!"

With rumblings about owner Thaksin Shinawatra being imprisoned for a number of crimes back in Thailand, the City owner's assets were eventually frozen. That didn't stop new boss Mark Hughes making some impressive new signings, with Vincent Kompany, Nigel de Jong, Shay Given, Pablo Zabaleta and Shaun Wright-Phillips, (who had been away for a few years at Chelsea), all joining City during the 2008/09 season. But there would be one more dramatic signing, and easily the most important development in the club's history, when it was announced the Abu Dhabi United Group, who had been in negotiations with Shinawatra's representatives, had purchased City in a deal reportedly worth £200m. The wealth of owner Sheikh Mansour bin Zayed Al Nahyan was vast – he was one of the richest men on the planet and, when the deal was signed and sealed, the highly respected Khaldoon Al Mubarak was installed as the new chairman.

There was no question mark against City's new owner who, in later Press reports, was identified as the ideal owner of any football club. City had struck gold – or in this case – oil!

The problem was there were just hours to go before the transfer window slammed shut so the Blues had to act quickly. There were reports of bids for Dimitar Berbatov, David Villa and Robinho but it would be only the latter, signed at a cost of £32.5m, who actually joined the club. United, dizzied by events across the city that they knew full well threatened their domination, were angry City tabled a bid for Berbatov, a player they had been courting for some time, but the message was clear: the gloves were off and City now had the financial muscle to compete with United.

It was the single most important shift in power since 1906 when Billy Meredith and Sandy Turnbull joined the Reds. For City fans it was the answer to all their prayers, while over at Old Trafford United fans wondered if this might be the beginning of the end of an era that had lasted the best part of 30 years. The answer, initially, was not a chance, but the new City owners saw their project as long term so were not in the least bit worried that there wasn't an immediate change of fortunes. They wanted to see progress but were realistic and patient. The Reds seemed to take inspiration from events across the city and the new season would see another incredible campaign take shape, and as far as they were concerned normal service was resumed by completing a derby double.

The first meeting of the 2008/09 season would be the first time the Manchester giants had met since the Blues had been taken over by the Abu Dhabi United Group, and there was now the real prospect that City would become a genuine title challenger in the near future.

The Reds were keen to throw a marker down, with the Blues champing at the bit to show their neighbours that they should indeed be worried, and had Stephen Ireland's shot gone in rather than striking the post, who knows what might have happened in this game? It seemed as though any immediate threat was a way off as United bossed the game at the City of Manchester Stadium and there was no real surprise when Wayne Rooney scored just before the break with his 100th career goal.

Robinho, City's own stellar talent, looked out of sorts and, at times, ill at ease in his weakest game since moving to England. He didn't seem to enjoy the physical side of the English game and barely a few months into his time with City it seemed defenders had sussed out that a few full-blooded challenges were enough to knock him out of his stride. There were times he looked as though he didn't want the ball in certain situations – a worrying development when the Blues had invested so much in his purchase.

Stephen Ireland and Shaun Wright-Phillips, City's other main attacking outlets, flickered sporadically and the home side did not really pose any threat until another Brazilian, Elano, came on at half-time. His introduction with Pablo Zabaleta was an admission on Hughes' part that the first half had been horribly one-sided. Rooney was having one of those days when he shimmered with menace every time he took the ball. Park Ji-Sung was busy and effective and Ronaldo started off in great form, always wanting the ball and full of positive running.

Rooney would be left to reflect on a hugely satisfying day's work, scoring the game's decisive moment after City's goalkeeper, Joe Hart, had parried Carrick's left-foot drive. For Ronaldo, however, everything would change during the space of 10 second-half minutes.

First of all he clipped Wright-Phillips' heels, cutting short a counter-attack and earning him his first yellow card from the referee Howard Webb. It could have turned into red if Webb had taken a dim view of Ronaldo sarcastically applauding the decision. Instead, his exit was sealed when Rooney swung over a corner and the Portugal star inexplicably decided to bat down the ball with both hands to earn his second red card against City in just a couple of years.

Why he did it only he will know. Ronaldo can be devastating in the air and the opportunity was there to have a go at goal. His argument was that Micah Richards had pushed him, but there was minimal contact, certainly not enough to make him lose the trajectory of the ball. He took an age to leave the pitch and, on the way, complained that he had tried to stop play after hearing what he thought was the referee's whistle. Again, it did not wash.

While the moment had brought a few smiles to the home support what they really wanted was a team who could go toe-to-toe with their neighbour and it was patently clear that was a long way off. The Blues' best chance came deep into injury time when Richard Dunne's effort was blocked on the goal line.

With United needing four points to guarantee the title City's trip to Old Trafford the following May was never going to be easy, particularly as they had only managed two wins on the road all season.

Squad rotation was an accepted part of life at United but Sir Alex Ferguson's team selection showed that he judged the level of risk in this match to be moderate at best.

The likes of Carrick and Rooney were on the bench while Rio Ferdinand, who had a calf strain, was not involved at all. Carlos Tevez was included but was not happy with the way his career with the Reds was going and, with no contract offer on the table, the Argentine felt more than a little aggrieved at the way things were panning out. His price tag was £22m and he felt he'd proved his worth but United were stalling and a permanent deal was in doubt.

Tevez would have to wait for his moment in the spotlight in the game, however, with Cristiano Ronaldo opening the scoring with a trademark free-kick after 18 minutes that wrong-footed Shay Given, and from there the result was never really in any doubt.

Tevez with a point to prove is a dangerous proposition for any team, so there was no real surprise when the former West Ham striker scored on this occasion. He had already swept inside Nedum Onuoha from the left and struck the far post in the 31st minute to serve Mark Hughes' side a warning, and on the stroke of half-time he doubled United's lead.

Darren Fletcher's pass found Dimitar Berbatov who played the ball into Tevez who made space for himself before firing home off the inside of the post.

City had no response of any note, with Robinho and Elano unable to conjure up any Brazilian magic to give their team a lifeline, and Hughes must have cast an envious glance at the unsettled Tevez and wondered, "what if…?" What if indeed!

The Reds, having already won the Carling Cup and with a Champions League final to look forward to, would seal the title at Wigan a few days later, while City prepared for another summer of team strengthening to close a gap that had been all too evident on this performance.

United would lose 2-0 to Barcelona in the showpiece of European club football but, having reached the semi-final of the FA Cup and added the Charity Shield too, this was one of United's best seasons on record. If it was a show of strength and defiance for their wealthy neighbours, who could only manage to finish 10th, it was a mightily impressive one.

During the summer of 2009 the Blues again demonstrated their buying power, bringing in Roque Santa Cruz, Emmanuel Adebayor, Kolo Touré, Gareth Barry and Joleon Lescott for a combined total of around £125m. The biggest transfer of the lot, however, also caused the most ill feeling between the two Manchester clubs when, in mid-July, City bought Carlos Tevez for £25m. Tevez had been on loan at Old Trafford for the previous two seasons but United were baulking at making the deal permanent so, when it became clear he was available, Mark Hughes wasted no time in making him a City player.

There was a new brash attitude about City – who had sensationally bid £100m for AC Milan's Kaka just six month earlier – and posters of Tevez in a mocked-up City shirt appeared around the city claiming "Welcome to Manchester", further infuriating United officials and supporters. Sir Alex tried to brush it all off, claiming the Blues had become "noisy neighbours", but he was rattled and perhaps could see that the threat from over the road was all too real.

Not only did United lose Tevez they also lost Cristiano Ronaldo to

Real Madrid for a world record fee of £80m to further weaken their strike force – what the Reds' fans were really concerned about was the fact that the money wasn't invested in the purchase of another stellar striker. Instead former Liverpool striker Michael Owen arrived on a free transfer and was joined by Wigan winger Antonio Valencia, but that was it.

When the season finally got underway the expectations at City were palpable, whereas United still felt they had more than enough in their locker to seal another title, and both Manchester clubs raced out of the blocks making the mid-September 2009 clash a top-of-the-table affair. It also ushered in a new dawn for the derby, with City fans going into the game expecting their team to at least test United's resolve; this clash was one of the best in years.

Rooney put the hosts ahead within two minutes, but City fought back through Barry just past the quarter-hour mark. Fletcher put United back in front shortly after half-time, but Craig Bellamy made it 2-2 with a fine individual goal just three minutes later. When Darren Fletcher nodded United ahead on 80 minutes it appeared that would be enough to take all three points, but Bellamy wasn't finished and neither were City. On 90 minutes the Welsh forward raced into the box, rounded the keeper and slotted home from an acute angle to send the City fans wild and make it 3-3 – but this exhilarating game still had one final twist and it came when Owen, written off by many United fans before he'd even kicked a ball, came off the bench to score a dramatic winner six minutes into injury time.

If this was the future of Manchester derbies then things were certainly looking up for a fixture that had desperately been in need of a jump-start. For Mark Hughes, though, it was to be his last as Manchester City manager, as he was sacked in December following a number of disappointing results: the Blues had drawn seven times in succession at one point and a demoralizing 3-0 defeat at Tottenham seemed to make up the minds of the Abu Dhabi owners that a change of direction was needed. Hughes had assembled a strong squad but it was decided a new man was needed to take the club to the next level – and that man was former Inter Milan boss Roberto Mancini.

Sir Alex had now seen off 16 different City managers and probably thought he could add his first Italian to that list – but Mancini was a proven winner in his own country and was a totally different proposition to any of the managers before him. With City and United paired together in the Carling Cup semi-final Mancini would have an early opportunity to show what he was capable of.

The first, at Eastlands, underlined the rediscovered passion for the derby in an explosive encounter. Ryan Giggs put United ahead on 17 minutes but a pumped-up Tevez and Bellamy were causing United all kinds of problems and, when Bellamy was felled in the box on 42 minutes, referee Mike Dean pointed to the spot and Tevez buried the ball past Edwin van der Sar to make it 1-1. Tevez ran towards Gary Neville who was warming up on the touchline and the Argentine celebrated in front of his former team-mate; the pair exchanged gestures and a few heated words – just what the Manchester derby is supposed to be like!

Just past the hour Tevez bravely nodded a second and ran to the centre circle, cupped his ears and stared towards the United bench. Needless to say the City fans lapped it up as their team took a deserved lead back to Old Trafford with them but, against this United team, it was a slender advantage to say the least.

City knew a solid, focused performance would see them at Wembley for the first time since the Gillingham 1999 Second Division play-off final. The Blues' determination to win silverware and kick-start a new era was almost tangible, but United, perhaps sensing a sea-change of power on the horizon, were determined to overturn the first-leg deficit and progress to the final where Aston Villa awaited the winners.

The tempo was high and the attacking intent undiluted, with each side employing a three-man forward line when in possession.

Rio Ferdinand was lucky to not give a penalty away on 24 minutes when he appeared to catch Carlos Tevez in the box, but Howard Webb decided there had been no foul and let play continue, much to the chagrin of the City players. Tevez forced Van der Sar into a good save on 30 minutes as the Blues searched for a breakthrough.

City held firm, going in marginally at the break the better side and still 2-1 ahead on aggregate. But seven minutes after the restart the Reds took the lead when Rooney picked out Ryan Giggs on the right and, after a challenge by Nani, the ball was laid back to Scholes by Michael Carrick. The veteran United midfielder drove home low past the right hand of Shay Given to level the aggregate at 2-2.

The Reds, for a time, threatened to swamp City with one attack after another, and the Blues were clinging on for dear life until Michael Carrick finally doubled United's lead on 71 minutes. The Blues looked down and out but when Carlos Tevez flicked home a volley not long after, it was suddenly game on again. With the match seemingly heading for extra time Wayne Rooney arrived on the right spot at exactly the right time to make it 3-1 with a fine header in front of the Stretford End. The majority of Old Trafford went wild.

It was an early lesson for new boss Mancini that United would take some shifting from their perch as Manchester's top team. With a handful of games to go City knew that if they won their remaining four games they would qualify for Champions League football for the first time (not including the old format European Cup which the Blues played just two games in). Standing in their way were United and fellow challengers for fourth spot, Tottenham.

The Blues also knew that if they could see off the Reds it would almost certainly ruin their hopes of winning the title, being four points behind leaders Chelsea going into the game. But the Reds had other ideas.

There could be no doubt that Sir Alex Ferguson had delivered some memorable dressing-room speeches during his Manchester United reign. Top of the list was the half-time address in the 1999 Champions League final when he inspired his players to their dramatic win by warning them of the agony of having to walk past the famous trophy if they lost.

And at Eastlands, against City, the rewards on the day may not have been as big, but the three points gained against the Blues at least kept alive hopes of a fourth successive Premier League title.

United skipper Gary Neville revealed how Fergie fired up his players in his pre-match address by questioning their desire to hold on to their title after their slip-ups against Chelsea and Blackburn.

"The manager asked us before the game 'Do you want to win this title?'" said Neville. "It may sound an obvious thing to ask, but the answer was 'yes, of course we do.'

"So we knew we had to go out and show our fans we have the pride and the desire to win matches – and to win the Premier League.

"We hope Chelsea will feel the negative effect of this win. They will have watched the game in their hotel before going to their match.

"All we can do is do our job and hope somebody does us a favour. And we're not getting carried away because we still have three difficult games to go."

Neville spoke before Spurs went on to record a rare win over Chelsea, meaning Paul Scholes' 93rd-minute winner against City reduced the gap at the top to just one point – as well as severely denting the Blues' Champions League aspirations.

The 35-year-old Scholes rolled back the years by timing his run to perfection and burying a header past Shay Given with just 17 seconds left. City just couldn't lift themselves in the bright Manchester sunshine and hopes of a top-four finish were all but extinguished. Worse still for City fans, this was the Reds' third injury-time victory over City in four games during the 2009/10 campaign.

Painful though it was for City it showed how far they had come in a short space of time and, in all four games, they had pushed United hard. A 1-0 defeat to Spurs meant Mancini's side finished fifth, with United missing out on the title by two points. But City were getting closer all the time...

Noisy Neighbours Turn Up the Volume

2011–2012

"On behalf of Manchester United I congratulate Manchester City on winning the Premier League. It's not an easy league to win and anyone who wins it deserves it, because it is a long haul."

Sir Alex Ferguson, 13th May 2012

City strengthened again in the summer bringing in Yaya Touré, James Milner, Mario Balotelli and Aleksandar Kolarov at a total cost approaching £90m. Edin Dzeko would join in January from Wolfsburg, too. The Reds' only notable signing was Mexican striker Javier Hernandez, otherwise United fans were disappointed at the club's American owners not opening the cheque book, particularly after they'd missed out on the Premier League and Champions League again. Sir Alex Ferguson's record, however, suggested he knew what he was doing, though he realized the gap between the Manchester clubs was closing fast. "We know the kind of money they're spending – they've bought another five or six players in the summer and they'll keep doing that until they win something. You know that's going to be the way it is and you have to deal with it as it comes along. They're up there, and you can't wait until tomorrow when there's something there today. I'm sure they're thinking that way themselves."

As it transpired, United made one of their best ever starts to a Premier League campaign and would remain unbeaten for their first 24 games – among them a sterile 0-0 draw at the City of Manchester Stadium.

For many, this was the derby that never was. A non-event in terms of entertainment and talking points, it was a poor advert for both of the Manchester clubs. What was crystal clear was that before a ball was even kicked, both managers – if not the players or supporters – would have taken 0-0, such was the desire not to lose this game.

Excitement was so restricted that an effort from City's Pablo Zabaleta, that went a little off target, brought the crowd briefly to life. Tevez had curled a good free-kick towards the top corner in the 35th minute but a goal would have needed a mistake by a well-positioned Edwin van der Sar to find the back of the net.

Given the extent of team rebuilding Roberto Mancini was undertaking, it was perhaps natural that he put the emphasis on establishing a measured approach rather than a gung-ho mentality that could, and probably would, have backfired.

But it was a risky move, with the Blues' tally of just 15 goals better only than West Brom and Blackpool at that point. United had a moment of menace when the substitute Wes Brown picked out Dimitar Berbatov after 57 minutes but the Bulgarian's volley flew straight to the goalkeeper, Hart. Brown had taken over from an injured Rafael da Silva, and the contest continued to find victims with Patrice Evra limping away and John O'Shea introduced instead.

The effort was evident but there was a lack of panache inside the box from both teams and a fairly turgid 0-0 draw was just about right on the night.

By mid-January City led the Premier League and were in with a chance of a first league title since 1968, but dropped points against Aston Villa and Birmingham meant they went into the February return derby at Old Trafford five points behind United and needing nothing less than a victory to get back in the title race.

As it was, a sensational winner from Wayne Rooney gave

Manchester United a dramatic 2-1 win and reminded City fans there was still some work to do to topple the Reds from a perch they'd sat undisturbed on for so long.

The Reds' surprise 2-1 defeat away to Wolves the previous week had been described as "pathetic" by Sir Alex Ferguson in the matchday programme, but he got the response he was looking for.

City played their part, too, with David Silva threatening throughout. Far from parking the bus, as had been suggested in the run-up to the game, the visitors had the chance to get the derby off to a sensational start after four minutes. A neat reverse pass from Tevez played in Silva who, with just Edwin van der Sar to beat, should still have done better than trickle a shot the wrong side of the post.

After that the game settled into a contest of attrition, with United rarely getting forward in numbers to support their lone striker and City showing more enterprise in attack but constantly losing the ball on the edge of the penalty area when intricate passing moves broke down.

The game was drifting uneventfully towards half-time when United made a route-one breakthrough. Joleon Lescott beat Rooney to Van der Sar's long clearance upfield but only knocked the ball into the path of Giggs who conjured a goal threat from almost nothing with an alert first-time pass to Nani. Bringing the ball down expertly the Portuguese winger held off Zabaleta to slip a low shot beyond Hart's left hand.

City hung in there and, midway through the second-half, Silva brought the scores level – though he did not know too much about it with the ball hitting his backside to deflect Dzeko's shot from a Wright-Phillips cross out of Van der Sar's reach.

The Blues could sense a surprise win, but United responded by sending on Dimitar Berbatov and immediately began to attack with increased confidence as more options opened up ahead. A terrific run by Nani took him slaloming past Zabaleta and then Vincent

Kompany, but ended with a wild shot, before the winger produced the assist from the right from which Rooney hit one of the goals of the season.

Meeting Nani's cross in mid-air, with his back to goal, Rooney gave Joe Hart no chance with the sort of finish he must have dreamed about as a boy. He celebrated in the corner with a flourish that an Olympic gymnast completing a floor exercise would have been proud of. With less than 10 minutes to play it was no surprise that the goal proved to be the winner and, grudgingly, even City fans would have been hard pressed to deny it hadn't been a goal worthy of winning any game.

"I thought we could go on to win from 1-1," said Mancini afterwards. "Then one fantastic goal changed everything."

Rooney, back in favour after his transfer request and subsequent about-turn a few weeks before, said: "I think it might have been the best goal I've ever scored. I'm pleased with the win; it was important after last week's result to keep that gap between ourselves and City."

Rooney's manager was even more impressed by it: "Absolutely stunning," Ferguson said. "Maybe the best goal I've ever seen here. It reminded me of Denis Law, though I don't know if even he could match that for execution."

Disappointing though it was City had given further evidence that the gulf in class had closed and the difference was now minimal. But that wasn't the end of the Manchester derby for the 2010/11 season – there was still one massive game to come – one of the biggest and highest-profile meetings between the two clubs ever – an FA Cup semi-final at Wembley Stadium.

Considering the Manchester clubs had never met in a major final, when the teams were drawn together it was fair to say it was the game neither wanted. In the other game Stoke City and Bolton Wanderers breathed a sigh of relief as at least one underdog would reach the final.

It seemed the whole of Manchester was at Wembley for the semi-final – with this a watershed moment for the Blues, who at last could see an end to the 35-year wait for silverware (if they could see off United). The Reds would have to do without the suspended Wayne Rooney, though rumours that Sir Alex Ferguson would field a weakened United side proved unfounded as the Reds' boss named something close to his strongest available team.

Dimitar Berbatov was preferred to Javier Hernandez in attack, while Roberto Mancini left Edin Dzeko on the bench and went with a front three comprising Adam Johnson, Mario Balotelli and David Silva. The formation was no surprise and neither was the absence of Carlos Tevez, who was still nursing an injury, and Vincent Kompany took over the captain's armband.

After 15 minutes of typically cagey semi-final action United suddenly burst into life and came close to taking the lead with a move that cut through the Blues' rear-guard with ease, and only Joe Hart's reactions denied Berbatov in the end. United nearly caught City out from the resultant throw-in, too, and were grateful Aleksandar Kolarov stayed alert at the far post to prevent Berbatov sliding home Nani's low cross.

Nemanja Vidic flashed a header wide from a corner as United began to rack up the goal attempts midway through the first half. By that point in the game City had offered little in the way of attacking, and their colourful and partisan following were living on their nerves. In fact, the first proper City threat didn't arrive until just past the half-hour mark when Silva's cross from the right picked out Balotelli near the penalty spot only for the ball to stick under the Italian's feet. Gareth Barry then shot from a narrow angle and could only find the side netting as the Blues finally sparked into life.

Mancini's men continued their best spell of the first half. Balotelli forced a save from Edwin van der Sar with a powerful effort from 30 yards out, then, from a Johnson corner, Joleon Lescott volleyed over at the far post from a position he probably would normally have hit the target from. City had ended the half on top, with Kompany going close and a good block from Vidic being required to stop a promising Yaya Touré – all of which boded well for the second period.

Then, seven minutes after the restart, one end of Wembley erupted. United made a series of defensive errors, starting with Van der Sar putting his own defenders under pressure with a weak clearance, then Carrick was muscled out by Touré who, with gathered momentum, held off Vidic before rolling a low shot beneath Van der Sar and into the net.

With United barely venturing out of their own half City relaxed to the extent of making a few trick passes as the hour came up, although what they really needed was another goal. Johnson almost forced an own goal from Van der Sar and Lescott headed wide from a Silva cross before United reminded their opponents that they were still in the game.

When Pablo Zabaleta was booked for bringing down Park the break in play was utilized to send on Hernandez for the disappointing Antonio Valencia then, from the free-kick just outside the area, Nani forced a fingertip save from Hart, who just managed to divert the ball onto his crossbar and out to safety.

United were to prove masters of their own downfall when Scholes, all too predictably, was given a straight red for a horror challenge on Pablo Zabaleta that raked the Argentina defender's thigh. In fairness, the ball was there to be won and neither player was holding back, but, whereas Zabaleta succeeded in reaching the ball, Scholes played only the man. City then comfortably played out the final 15 minutes or so to record a famous win and progress to their first FA Cup final for 30 years. They had looked the better team for two thirds of the game and, on the day, United were disappointing and clearly missing the fire and brimstone Rooney brought with him.

"I am very happy for our supporters, because they deserve this," said a jubilant Roberto Mancini. "It is important to start winning trophies, and I stand by my claim that if we win the FA Cup this year we can try for the title next season. This could be a turning point for us but it is important to remember there is another game to win. I think we can go on from this to win the FA Cup and secure a top-four finish."

Meanwhile, United made it a Manchester double by securing a record 20th top-flight title – an incredible achievement that quite rightly earned the Reds plenty of plaudits. It was also a show of defiance that Sir Alex Ferguson's men were far from a spent force!

The Reds also still had the Champions League final to look forward to as well but, again, they faced a Lionel Messi-inspired Barcelona and would lose 3-1. What a season for Manchester football fans, who could confidently now claim to have two footballing superpowers.

The Blues reckoned the new campaign might just be the one that finally ended 44 years of waiting for a league title, and Sergio Aguero and Samir Nasri were added to the mix as Mancini fine-tuned his squad. United added Phil Jones, Ashley Young and goalkeeper David de Gea in response, and there wasn't long to wait for the first City vs United clash of the season – the traditional curtain raiser: the Community Shield.

In a thrilling five-goal thriller City saw a two-goal lead slip against United as Sir Alex Ferguson's side threw the first gauntlet down.

Starting the new season with a Manchester derby at Wembley was a new experience, but one every City fan could get used to. With the early morning sunshine giving way to drizzle by kick-off the greasy pitch was initially handled better by United, whose passing was crisper and more accurate in the opening stages, leading to a couple of goal-mouth scrambles that could have resulted in a goal.

The Blues, just as they had done in the FA Cup semi-final against the Reds, gradually played their way into the game and, as the tackles flew in from either side and yellow cards began to flow, it soon underlined that this was far more than just a showpiece curtain raiser; seven minutes before the break, the match finally had its first goal.

Milner's dashing run was halted by Patrice Evra on the edge of the box. From the resulting free-kick Silva's pinpoint cross found Lescott who glanced the ball past De Gea to send the City fans wild.

While the Poznan was still shaking the Wembley foundations, the Blues went 2-0 up as Mancini's side began to pick United apart at will. This time it was Edin Dzeko who once again sent the Blue Army into raptures when he let fly a 30-yard thunderbolt on the stroke of half-time.

Having established some breathing space it was crucial City keep United at bay for at least the opening 20 minutes of the second half but, instead, slack marking allowed Chris Smalling the chance to guide Ashley Young's cross past Joe Hart with just 52 minutes on the clock.

There was worse to follow for the Blues six minutes later as United drew level when Nani worked his way through to chip the ball over Hart from close range and, with 30 minutes still to play, City were hanging on.

As United swarmed forward City managed to repel a series of attacks that threatened to engulf Mancini's side at one point, but it was Nani – again – who ensured the first piece of silverware this season went to Old Trafford and not the Etihad Stadium with a coolly taken winner that sent the United fans delirious. Rarely had a Community Shield game been played with such passion or the goals been celebrated with such wild abandon – it was the perfect start to what would be the most dramatic Premier League campaign ever.

There would be three more Manchester derbies in the 2011/12 season and each one would have its own drama and excitement. It would also be the first time since 1968 that the two city rivals would go head to head for the title in an incredible season.

The first derby of the campaign took place at Old Trafford in October and was nothing short of sensational. City went into the game two points clear of the Reds, having won seven of their first eight games, but whatever City did United matched in a breath-taking start. Both derbies could have a critical bearing on who won the league, but nobody could have predicted just what an impact this game would have on the title race. This was a game that, claimed the Press, United fans would have recurring nightmares of for generations.

It was a day when everything went right for City as a message was sent out to the rest of the Premier League that the champions might just come from the blue half of the city this time around.

Mario Balotelli was preferred to Edin Dzeko up front and it was the Italian's sublime finish at the Stretford End that opened the scoring on 22 minutes – the fifth consecutive time he'd found the net for the Blues.

Silva picked out James Milner, and the low ball to the edge of the area from the left was converted with great precision by Balotelli, who shot past the left hand of the goalkeeper David de Gea. He then lifted his shirt to reveal a T-shirt with the message "Why always me?"

The game arguably turned after just 46 minutes when Balotelli slipped the attentions of Jonny Evans who then pulled the City striker back when through on goal to leave the referee with an easy decision to send Evans off. Suddenly United's task had become that much tougher and, just after the hour, with Silva orchestrating the midfield, City scored again.

A flowing move saw Silva turn and unleash Milner inside the penalty area whose cross found Aguero at the far post to knock the ball into the net. Then a combination of Milner and Micah Richards set Balotelli up for his second shortly after, with the Blues cutting the home defence to shreds, seemingly, at will.

Darren Fletcher pulled one back with 10 minutes to go but City were still completely in command and, with normal time up, it seemed that was just about that – only City were far from finished. United adopted a cavalier attitude to the closing stages, perhaps hoping one more goal might unnerve their neighbours, but it was foolhardy at best with Silva in scintillating form, and the Blues took full advantage of the space afforded to them. First a delicious Silva pass sent Dzeko clear to make it 4-1, then Silva capped off a memorable performance with the fifth, before Dzeko completed the rout shortly after – City had scored three goals in added time to record their highest win at Old Trafford since 23rd January 1926.

It was also Sir Alex Ferguson's heaviest defeat in his 25-year tenure and he couldn't quite believe what he'd seen. "It was our worst ever day. It's the worst result in my history, ever. Even as a player I don't think I ever lost 6-1. I can't believe the scoreline. I'm shattered. It's an incredible disappointment."

Not a great way to celebrate 25 years as United boss!

The result sent shockwaves through football and the City fans enjoyed the moment to the full – and who could blame them? Texts were sent, T-shirts printed and jokes created, and why not? But there was still a long, long way to go and United responded magnificently, never letting City increase their lead at the top by more than five, and winning matches by whatever means necessary. It was a fascinating duel, with the Reds clearly taking inspiration from their neighbours' endeavours. Perhaps the thought of handing the Premier League trophy over to City was making what was generally accepted to be a so-so Reds team punch above their weight?

When the teams were paired together for the FA Cup-tie's third round United were presented with a chance to get some instant payback with a first meeting at the newly christened Etihad Stadium – and they took it and, at one point, seemed to be heading for a six-goal win of their own.

Five goals, a red card, controversy and a grandstand finish – for the neutral this was the FA Cup back to its very best, but there had to be a loser on the day and the victors knew it could possibly give them an important psychological advantage going into the final months of the season.

Though United were more than a match for City on the day, referee Chris Foy's decision to send off skipper Vincent Kompany, after just 12 minutes for what was deemed a two-footed lunge on Nani, who didn't even appeal for a foul, may have skewered events somewhat – though the outcome of the match had both sides had 11 players will never be known.

United fans will point to the fact Wayne Rooney opened the scoring two minutes before Kompany saw red, with a superb header from Antonio Valencia's cross on 10 minutes, and when Danny Welbeck acrobatically volleyed home past stand-in keeper Costel Pantilimon, to make it 2-0, the Blues looked as good as out of the competition they were defending champions of. Worse still for City fans: Rooney's penalty, initially saved by Pantilimon but converted on the follow-up, made it 3-0 and there was a very real chance United would exact full revenge for the 6-1 defeat in October with a demolition derby of their own.

But, against all odds, some astute tactical manoeuvring by Roberto Mancini saw City re-adjusted to 3-5-1 and immediately United were troubled and, when Aleks Kolarov's 25-yard free-kick curled past the defensive wall and beat Anders Lindegaard, the hosts could see a chink of light.

City suddenly had United on the ropes and reduced the deficit further when Sergio Aguero met James Milner's low ball to score the Blues' second. United were paying the price for sitting back on their three-goal cushion and, had Aguero's injury-time effort gone in, they may even have had to face the prospect of an Old Trafford derby with the wounds of the previous one not even starting to heal.

A strange game where both teams took something from the game, but only the Reds progressed to the fourth round.

In the final two months of the campaign United's relentless pursuit of City finally paid off as they drew level and then went eight points clear of Roberto Mancini's men with just six games to go.

Both managers were guilty of playing mind games but, for probably the first time anyone could remember, Mancini became one of the few – maybe even the first – to get inside Sir Alex's head. Whenever asked if City could still win the title – and particularly after a 1-0 defeat to Arsenal left City eight points adrift and just six games remaining – the Blues boss would say, "No, the title is over."

The Blues looked as though they were, in effect, as good as out of the race, but privately refused to throw in the towel. With the return league derby still to come, there was still hope.

It was around this point that thousands of United fans felt safe enough to send their City friends and family members mocking texts about how the noisy neighbours had suddenly gone quiet and other disparaging comments about how the situation had switched around – plus how amusing it all was to the Reds; but those who sent messages out would ultimately regret doing so.

The impossible dream began to seem possible: United threw points away against Wigan Athletic and then dropped two more against Everton, while the Blues won their next three games. Suddenly, a win over the Reds at the Etihad meant the title was back in City's hands. It was an unbelievable turnaround – the question was would City take their opportunity? The answer was an emphatic "yes". The biggest Manchester derby of all time really was a winner-takes-all affair. A cagey first 45 was drawing to a close when the Blues won a corner deep into first-half stoppage time. As David Silva prepared to deliver the cross David de Gea was crucially distracted by the presence of Carlos Tevez so, when Vincent Kompany lost his marker, Chris Smalling, the Spanish keeper was powerless to prevent the City skipper scoring the opening goal of the game – it would also prove to be the only goal of the game.

Driven on by the remarkable Yaya Touré the side that was written off by most, including Roberto Mancini just a few weeks before, now found themselves just two victories from glory.

Sir Alex Ferguson's decision to clip his own team's wings and leave the dangerous Antonio Valencia and Ashley Young on the bench proved fatal, and United did not have a shot on target as they appeared to go against their own instincts by not going for the jugular.

City waited for the expected backlash after the break but, in truth, it never came. Apart from the odd threat City were far more composed and carried more menace in attack. Ferguson unleashed the attacking trio of Danny Welbeck, Valencia and Young in the closing stages, but to no avail.

Nigel de Jong's clumsy tackle on Welbeck resulted in a furious Ferguson and Mancini exchange with fourth official Mike Jones intervening between the pair before each was dragged away – passions were running high. City were now level on points, but with a far superior goal difference – in short, destiny was back in the Blues' hands. It was nothing short of sensational.

The title race went to the last kick of the season, with both teams winning their next game and going into the final game of the campaign on level points.

Yet, with City at home to relegation threatened QPR and United at Sunderland, it seemed nothing could stop Roberto Mancini becoming the first manager of the Blues to deliver the title since Joe Mercer in 1968.

The events of 13th May 2012 are now etched into Premier League history, with so many twists and turns over the course of 90 minutes. The Reds struck first, meaning City had to win unless things changed at the Stadium of Light, and it wasn't until just before the break that the Blues finally broke the deadlock against QPR, with Pablo Zabaleta putting his side ahead.

City were far from their best and the Etihad Stadium could sense their team's apprehension. After the break QPR held firm and then, when Joleon Lescott misjudged a high ball, Djibril Cissé hit a powerful low shot past Joe Hart. The title, as things stood, was going to Old Trafford. But there was more drama to come when Jamie Mackie nodded the Hoops ahead on 71 minutes to stun the home support. City, now 2-1 down and, as it stood, three points behind the Reds, threw everything forward, but time was ticking on and it seemed it just wasn't going to be their day. As the board went up to show five minutes of added time City poured forward again, more in hope now than belief. Then Dzeko headed a Silva corner home and City had three minutes to win their first Premier League title – it was as simple as that.

News came through that United had won 1-0 and their players were on the pitch at the Stadium of Light waiting to hear if City had blown it. Then, with the 95 minutes almost up, Nigel de Jong played the ball to Aguero who played it to Balotelli. The Italian managed to return the ball to the Argentinian who feigned to shoot, skipped around a defender and slammed the ball home to make it 3-2. The Etihad Stadium went crazy and City had won the title. It was pure Hollywood and, painful as it was for United, they had played their part to the full. The news broke on a thousand radios and phones at Sunderland and, while the home fans mocked the United players, realization sank in that it was City's day after all and a crestfallen Sir Alex ushered his team to go and thank their supporters.

It had taken a long, long time, but the Blues had finally made it.

So what next? City won't be going away and will be challenging for the title for many years to come. The question is how will United respond? They're certainly not going to fade away and let the Blues dominate English football.

We'll let Sir Alex Ferguson and Roberto Mancini have the last words. Sir Alex warned: "City aren't going anywhere, but nor am I. This is our latest challenge and we'll just have to accept it."

Mancini said: "Any team that finishes above United and beats them home and away in the same season deserves to win the title. United are a fantastic side and our aim is to try and achieve the success they have had over the years. That is our goal."

Whichever side of the city your allegiance is to nobody can deny – even the staunchest Red or most loyal Blue – that Manchester is blessed with two of the most famous, colourful and entertaining football clubs in the world. Just as it was in the late 1960s, Manchester is once again the football capital of the world and the bottom line is, despite what we say to others, the world would be a duller place without the Manchester derby.

The rivalry has never been greater and the football never better. Manchester is the place to be and the derby really is the only game in town. Exactly how it should be…

Now, what happens next…? Watch this space!

The Complete Record

1891/92

FA Cup, 3rd October 1891

Newton Heath 5   **Ardwick 1**

Sneddon   Pearson

Doughty, Farman (2), Edge

Venue: North Road

Attendance: 11,000

1892/9

No game

1893/94

No game

1894/95

Division Two, 3rd November 1894

Manchester City 2   **Newton Heath 5**

Meredith (2)   Smith (4)

                                Clarkin

Venue: Hyde Road

Attendance: 14,000

Division Two, 5th January 1895

Newton Heath 4   **Manchester City 1**

Clarkin (2)   Sharples

Donaldson, Smith

Venue: Clayton

Attendance: 12,000

1895/96

Division Two, 5th October 1895

Newton Heath 1   **Manchester City 1**

Clarkin   Rowan

Venue: Clayton

Attendance: 12,000

Division Two, 7th December 1895

Manchester City 2   **Newton Heath 1**

Hill   Cassidy

Meredith

Venue: Hyde Road

Attendance: 18,000

1896/97

Division Two, 3rd October 1896

Manchester City 0   **Newton Heath 0**

Venue: Hyde Road

Attendance: 20,000

Division Two, 25th December 1896

Newton Heath 2   **Manchester City 1**

Smith, Donaldson   Hill

Venue: Clayton

Attendance: 18,000

1897/98

Division Two, 16th October 1897

Newton Heath 1   **Manchester City 1**

Gillespie   Hill

Venue: Clayton

Attendance: 20,000

Division Two, 25th December 1897

Manchester City 0   **Newton Heath 1**

                                      Cassidy

Venue: Hyde Road

Attendance: 16,000

1898/99

Division Two, 10th September 1898

Newton Heath 3   **Manchester City 0**

Cassidy (2, 1 pen)

Boyd

Venue: Clayton

Attendance: 20,000

Division Two, 26th December 1898

Manchester City 4   **Newton Heath 0**

F Williams

Meredith

Gillespie

Dougal

Venue: Hyde Road

Attendance: 25,000

1899/1900

No game

1900/01

No game

1901/02

No game

1902/03

Division Two, 25th December 1902

Manchester United 1   **Manchester City 1**

Pegg   Meredith

Venue: Clayton
Attendance: 40,000

Division Two, 10th April 1903

Manchester City 0   **Manchester United 2**

Holmes (o.g.)

Schofield

Venue: Hyde Road
Attendance: 30,000

1903/04

No game

1904/05

No game

1905/06

No game

1906/07

Division One, 1st December 1906

Manchester City 3   **Manchester United 0**

Stewart (2)

Jones

Venue: Hyde Road

Attendance: 40,000

Division One, 6th April 1907

Manchester United 1   **Manchester City 1**

Roberts   Dorsett (pen)

Venue: Clayton

Attendance: 40,000

1907/08

Division One, 21st December 1907

Manchester United 3   **Manchester City 1**

Wall   Eadie

Turnbull (2)

Venue: Clayton

Attendance: 35,000

Division One, 18th April 1908

Manchester City 0   **Manchester United 0**

Venue: Hyde Road

Attendance: 40,000

1908/09

Division One, 19th September 1908

Manchester City 1   **Manchester United 2**

Thornley   J Turnbull

                               Halse

Venue: Hyde Road

Attendance: 40,000

Division One, 23rd January 1909

Manchester United 3   **Manchester City 1**

Livingstone (2)   Conlin

Wall

Venue: Clayton

Attendance: 40,000

1909/10

No game

1910/11

Division One, 17th September 1910

Manchester United 2   **Manchester City 1**

West   Jones

Turnbull

Venue: Old Trafford

Attendance: 60,000

Division One, 21st January 1911

Manchester City 1   **Manchester United 1**

Jones   Turnbull

Venue: Hyde Road

Attendance: 40,000

1911/12

Division One, 2nd September 1911

Manchester City 0   **Manchester United 0**

Venue: Hyde Road

Attendance: 35,000

Division One, 30th December 1911

Manchester United 0   **Manchester City 0**

Venue: Old Trafford
Attendance: 50,000

1912/13

Division One, 7th September 1912

Manchester United 0   **Manchester City 1**
                             Wynn

Venue: Old Trafford
Attendance: 38,911

Division One, 28th December 1912

Manchester City 0   **Manchester United 2**
                          West (2)

Venue: Hyde Road
Attendance: 36,223

1913/14

Division One, 6th December 1913

Manchester City 0   **Manchester United 2**
                          Anderson (2)

Venue: Hyde Road
Attendance: 36,223

Division One, 11th April 1914

Manchester United 0   **Manchester City 1**
                             Cumming

Venue: Old Trafford
Attendance: 36,440

1914/15

Division One, 5th September 1914

Manchester United 0   **Manchester City 0**

Venue: Old Trafford

Attendance: 20,000

Division One, 2nd January 1915

Manchester City 1   **Manchester United 1**

Howard   West

Venue: Hyde Road

Attendance: 30,000

1915/16

No game

1916/17

No game

1917/18

No game

1918/19

No game

1919/20

Division One, 11th October 1919

Manchester City 3   **Manchester United 3**

Taylor   Hodge

Browell (2)   Spence

                          Hopkin

Venue: Hyde Road

Attendance: 32,000

Division One, 18th October 1919
Manchester United 1   **Manchester City 0**
Spence
Venue: Old Trafford
Attendance: 49,000

1920/21

Division One, 20th November 1920
Manchester United 1   **Manchester City 1**
Miller   Barnes
Venue: Old Trafford
Attendance: 63,000

Division One, 27th November 1920
Manchester City 3   **Manchester United 0**
Barnes
Browell
Murphy
Venue: Hyde Road
Attendance: 40,000

1921/22

Division One, 22nd October 1921
Manchester City 4   **Manchester United 1**
Barnes (3, 1 pen)   Spence
Warner
Venue: Hyde Road
Attendance: 20,000

Division One, 29th October 1921
Manchester United 3   **Manchester City 1**
Spence (3)   Murphy

Venue: Old Trafford
Attendance: 56,000

1922/23

No game

1923/24

No game

1924/25

No game

1925/26

Division One, 12th September 1925
Manchester City 1   **Manchester United 1**
Cowan   Rennox
Venue: Maine Road
Attendance: 62,994

Division One, 23rd January 1926
Manchester United 1   **Manchester City 6**
Rennox   Roberts (2)
                               Austin (2)
                               Johnson
                               Hicks

Venue: Old Trafford
Attendance: 48,657

FA Cup, 27th March 1926
Manchester City 3   **Manchester United 0**
Browell (2)
Roberts

Venue: Bramall Lane, Sheffield
Attendance: 46,450

1926/27

No game

1927/28

No game

1928/29

Division One, 1st September 1928

Manchester City 2   **Manchester United 2**

Roberts   Wilson

Johnson   Johnston

Venue: Maine Road
Attendance: 61,007

Division One, 5th January 1929

Manchester United 1   **Manchester City 2**

Rawlings   Austin

                               Johnson

Venue: Old Trafford
Attendance: 42,555

1929/30

Division One, 5th October 1929

Manchester United 1   **Manchester City 3**

Thomas   Johnson

                               Marshall

                               Brook

Venue: Old Trafford
Attendance: 57,201

Division One, 8th February 1930

Manchester City 0   **Manchester United 1**

Reid

Venue: Maine Road
Attendance: 64,472

1930/31

Division One, 4th October 1930

Manchester City 4   **Manchester United 1**

Tait (2)   Spence

Marshall (2)

Venue: Maine Road
Attendance: 41,757

Division One, 7th February 1931

Manchester United 1   **Manchester City 3**

Spence   Brook

Toseland

Halliday

Venue: Old Trafford
Attendance: 39,876

1931/32

No game

1932/33

No game

1933/34

No game

1934/35

No game

1935/36

No game

1936/37

Division One, 12th September 1936

Manchester United 3   **Manchester City 2**

Bamford   Bray

Manley   Heale

Bryant

Venue: Old Trafford

Attendance: 68,796

Division One, 9th January 1937

Manchester City 1   **Manchester United 0**

Herd

Venue: Maine Road

Attendance: 62,895

1937/38

No game

1938/39

No game

1939–46

No games due to the Second World War

1946/47

Back to league format: No game

1947/48

Division One, 20th September 1947

Manchester City 0   **Manchester United 0**

Venue: Maine Road
Attendance: 78,000

Division One, 7th April 1948

Manchester United 1   **Manchester City 1**

Rowley   Linacre

Venue: Maine Road*
Attendance: 71,690

*Start of Manchester United using Maine Road as their temporary home

1948/49

Division One, 11th September 1948

Manchester City 0   **Manchester United 0**

Venue: Maine Road
Attendance: 64,502

Division One, 22nd January 1949

Manchester United 0   **Manchester City 0**

Venue: Maine Road
Attendance: 66,485

1949/50

Division One, 20th September 1949

Manchester United 2   **Manchester City 1**

Pearson (2)   Munro

Venue: Old Trafford
Attendance: 47,706

Division One, 31ˢᵗ December 1949

Manchester City 1   **Manchester United 2**

Black   Delaney

                               Pearson

Venue: Maine Road

Attendance: 63,704

1950/51

No game

1951/52

Division One, 5ᵗʰ September 1951

Manchester City 1   **Manchester United 2**

Hart   Berry

                               McShane

Venue: Maine Road

Attendance: 52,571

Division One, 19ᵗʰ January 1952

Manchester United 1   **Manchester City 1**

Carey   McCourt

Venue: Old Trafford

Attendance: 54,245

1952/53

Division One, 30ᵗʰ August 1952

Manchester City 2   **Manchester United 1**

Clarke   Downie

Broadis

Venue: Maine Road

Attendance: 56,140

Division One, 3rd January 1953

Manchester United 1   **Manchester City 1**

Pearson   Broadis

Venue: Old Trafford

Attendance: 47,883

1953/54

Division One, 5th September 1953

Manchester City 2   **Manchester United 0**

Hart, Revie

Venue: Maine Road

Attendance: 53,097

Division One, 16th January 1954

Manchester United 1   **Manchester City 1**

Berry   McAdams

Venue: Old Trafford

Attendance: 46,379

1954/55

Division One, 25th September 1954

Manchester City 3   **Manchester United 2**

McAdams   Taylor

Fagan   Blanchflower

Hart

Venue: Maine Road

Attendance: 54,105

FA Cup, 29th January 1955
Manchester City 2   **Manchester United 0**
Hayes
Revie
Venue: Maine Road
Attendance: 74,723

Division One, 12th February 1955
Manchester United 0   **Manchester City 5**
                                  Hart
                                  Fagan (2)
                                  Hayes (2)
Venue: Old Trafford
Attendance: 47,914

1955/56

Division One, 3rd September 1955
Manchester City 1   **Manchester United 0**
Hayes
Venue: Maine Road
Attendance: 59,192

Division One, 31st December 1955
Manchester United 2   **Manchester City 1**
Taylor   Dyson
Viollet
Venue: Old Trafford
Attendance: 60,956

1956/57

Division One, 22nd September 1956
Manchester United 2   **Manchester City 0**

Viollet

Whelan

Venue: Old Trafford

Attendance: 53,515

Charity Shield, 24th October 1956

Manchester City 0   **Manchester United 1**

                                   Viollet

Venue: Maine Road

Attendance: 30,495

Division One, 2nd February 1957

Manchester City 2   **Manchester United 4**

Clarke   Whelan

Hayes   Taylor

                                     Viollet

                                     Edwards

Venue: Maine Road

Attendance: 63,872

1957/58

Division One, 31st August 1957

Manchester United 4   **Manchester City 1**

Edwards   Barnes

Berry

Viollet

Taylor

Venue: Old Trafford

Attendance: 63,103

Division One, 28th December 1957

Manchester City 2   **Manchester United 2**

Hayes   Viollet

Foulkes (o.g.)   Charlton

Venue: Maine Road

Attendance: 70,493

1958/59

Division One, 27th September 1958

Manchester City 1   **Manchester United 1**

Hayes   Charlton (pen)

Venue: Maine Road

Attendance: 62,812

Division One, 14th February 1959

Manchester United 4   **Manchester City 1**

Goodwin   Johnstone

Bradley (2)

Scanlon

Venue: Old Trafford

Attendance: 59,604

1959/60

Division One, 19th September 1959

Manchester City 3   **Manchester United 0**

Hayes (2)

Hannah

Venue: Maine Road

Attendance: 58,300

Division One, 6th February 1960

Manchester United 0   **Manchester City 0**

Venue: Old Trafford

Attendance: 59,450

1960/61

Division One, 31st December 1960

Manchester United 5   **Manchester City 1**

Charlton (2)

Dawson (3)   Barlow

Venue: Old Trafford

Attendance: 61,213

Division One, 4th March 1961

Manchester City 1   **Manchester United 3**

Wagstaffe   Dawson, Charlton, Pearson

Venue: Maine Road

Attendance: 50,479

1961/62

Division One, 23rd September 1961

Manchester United 3   **Manchester City 2**

Stiles   Stiles (o.g.)

Viollet   Kennedy

Ewing (o.g.)

Venue: Old Trafford

Attendance: 55,933

Division One, 10th February 1962

Manchester City 0   **Manchester United 2**

                                Chisnall

                                Herd

Venue: Maine Road

Attendance: 49,959

1962/63

Division One, 15th September 1962

Manchester United 2   **Manchester City 3**

Law (2)   Dobing (pen)

                                 Hayes

                                 Harley

Venue: Old Trafford

Attendance: 49,193

Division One, 15th May 1963

Manchester City 1   **Manchester United 1**

Harley   Quixall (pen)

Venue: Maine Road

Attendance: 52,424

1963/64

No game

1964/65

No game

1965/66

No game

1966/67

Division One, 17th September 1966

Manchester United 1   **Manchester City 0**

Law

Venue: Old Trafford

Attendance: 62,085

Division One, 21st January 1967

Manchester City 1   **Manchester United 1**

Stiles (o.g.)   Foulkes

Venue: Maine Road

Attendance: 62,983

1967/68

Division One, 30th September 1967

Manchester City 1   **Manchester United 2**

Bell   Charlton (2)

Venue: Maine Road

Attendance: 62,942

Division One, 27th March 1968

Manchester United 1   **Manchester City 3**

Best   Bell

                                    Heslop

                                    Lee (pen)

Venue: Old Trafford

Attendance: 63,004

1968/69

Division One, 17th August 1968

Manchester City 0   **Manchester United 0**

Venue: Maine Road

Attendance: 63,052

Division One, 21st January 1969

Manchester United 0   **Manchester City 1**

                                    Summerbee

Venue: Old Trafford

Attendance: 63,388

1969/70

Division One, 15th November 1969

Manchester City 4   **Manchester United 0**

Young

Bell (2)

Sadler (o.g.)

Venue: Maine Road

Attendance: 63,013

League Cup Semi-final (first leg), 3rd December 1969

Manchester City 2   **Manchester United 1**

Bell   Charlton

Lee (pen)

Venue: Maine Road

Attendance: 55,799

League Cup Semi-final (second leg), 17th December 1969

Manchester United 2   **Manchester City 2**

Edwards   Bowyer

Law   Summerbee

Venue: Old Trafford

Attendance: 63,418

(Manchester City win 4-3 on aggregate)

FA Cup, 24th January 1970

Manchester United 3   **Manchester City 0**

Morgan (pen)

Kidd (2)

Venue: Old Trafford

Attendance: 63,417

Division One, 28th March 1970

Manchester United 1   **Manchester City 2**

Kidd   Lee (pen)

                          Doyle

Venue: Old Trafford
Attendance: 60,286

1970/71

Division One, 12th December 1970

Manchester United 1   **Manchester City 4**

Kidd   Doyle

                          Lee (3)

Venue: Old Trafford
Attendance: 52,636

Division One, 5th May 1971

Manchester City 3   **Manchester United 4**

Hill   Charlton

Mellor   Law

Lee   Best (2)

Venue: Maine Road
Attendance: 43,636

1971/72

Division One, 6th November 1971

Manchester City 3   **Manchester United 3**

Lee (pen)   McIlroy

Bell   Kidd

Summerbee   Gowling

Venue: Maine Road
Attendance: 63,326

Division One, 12th April 1972

Manchester United 1   **Manchester City 3**

Buchan   Lee (2)

                                                       Marsh

Venue: Old Trafford

Attendance: 56,362

1972/73

Division One, 18th November 1972

Manchester City 3   **Manchester United 0**

Bell (2)

Buchan (o.g.)

Venue: Maine Road

Attendance: 52,050

Division One, 21st April 1973

Manchester United 0   **Manchester City 0**

Venue: Old Trafford

Attendance: 61,676

1973/74

Division One, 12th March 1974

Manchester City 0   **Manchester United 0**

Venue: Maine Road

Attendance: 51,331

Division One, 21st April 1974

Manchester United 0   **Manchester City 1**

                                                       Law

Venue: Old Trafford

Attendance: 56,996

1974/75

League Cup Fourth Round, 9th October 1974

Manchester United 1   **Manchester City 0**

Daly (pen)

Venue: Old Trafford

Attendance: 55,169

1975/76

Division One, 27th September 1975

Manchester City 2   **Manchester United 2**

Nicholl (o.g.)   McCreery

Royle   Macari

Venue: Maine Road

Attendance: 46,931

League Cup Fourth Round, 12th November 1975

Manchester City 4   **Manchester United 0**

Tueart (2)

Hartford

Royle

Venue: Maine Road

Attendance: 50,182

Division One, 4th May 1976

Manchester United 2   **Manchester City 0**

McIlroy

Hill

Venue: Old Trafford

Attendance: 58,528

1976/77

Division One, 25th September 1976

Manchester City 1   **Manchester United 3**

Tueart   Coppell

                               McCreery

                               Daly

Venue: Maine Road

Attendance: 48,861

Division One, 5th March 1977

Manchester United 3   **Manchester City 1**

Pearson   Tueart

Hill

Coppell

Venue: Old Trafford

Attendance: 58,595

1977/78

Division One, 10th September 1977

Manchester City 3   **Manchester United 1**

Kidd (2)   Nicholl

Channon

Venue: Maine Road

Attendance: 50,856

Division One, 15th March 1978

Manchester United 2   **Manchester City 2**

Hill 2 (2 pens)   Barnes

                                 Kidd

Venue: Old Trafford

Attendance: 58,398

1978/79

Division One, 30th September 1978

Manchester United 1   **Manchester City 0**

Jordan

Venue: Old Trafford

Attendance: 55,301

Division One, 10th February 1979

Manchester City 0   **Manchester United 3**

Coppell (2)

Ritchie

Venue: Maine Road

Attendance: 46,151

1979/80

Division One, 10th November 1979

Manchester City 2   **Manchester United 0**

Henry

Robinson

Venue: Maine Road

Attendance: 50,067

Division One, 22nd March 1980

Manchester United 1   **Manchester City 0**

Thomas

Venue: Old Trafford

Attendance: 56,387

1980/81

Division One, 27th September 1980

Manchester United 2   **Manchester City 2**

Coppell   Reeves

Albiston   Palmer
Venue: Old Trafford
Attendance: 55,918

Division One, 21st February 1981
Manchester City 1   **Manchester United 0**
MacKenzie
Venue: Maine Road
Attendance: 50,114

1981/82

Division One, 10th October 1981
Manchester City 0   **Manchester United 0**
Venue: Maine Road
Attendance: 52,037

Division One, 27th February 1982
Manchester United 1   **Manchester City 1**
Moran   Reeves
Venue: Old Trafford
Attendance: 57,830

1982/83

Division One, 23rd October 1982
Manchester United 2   **Manchester City 2**
Stapleton (2)   Tueart
                               Cross
Venue: Old Trafford
Attendance: 57,334

Division One, 5th March 1983
Manchester City 1   **Manchester United 2**

Reeves   Stapleton (2)
Venue: Maine Road
Attendance: 45,400

1983/84
No game

1984/85
No game

1985/86
Division One, 14th September 1985
Manchester City 0   **Manchester United 3**
                             Robson (pen)
                             Albiston
                             Duxbury
Venue: Maine Road
Attendance: 48,773

Division One, 22nd March 1986
Manchester United 2   **Manchester City 2**
Gibson   Wilson
Strachan (pen)   Albiston (o.g.)
Venue: Old Trafford
Attendance: 51,274

1986/87
Division One, 26th October 1986
Manchester City 1   **Manchester United 1**
McCarthy   Stapleton
Venue: Maine Road
Attendance: 32,440

FA Cup Third Round, 10th January 1987

Manchester United 1   **Manchester City 0**

Whiteside

Venue: Old Trafford

Attendance: 54,294

Division One, 7th March 1987

Manchester United 2   **Manchester City 0**

Reid (o.g.)

Robson

Venue: Old Trafford

Attendance: 48,619

1987/88

No game

1988/89

No game

1989/90

Division One, 23rd September 1989

Manchester City 5   **Manchester United 1**

Oldfield (2)   Hughes

Morley

Bishop

Hinchcliffe

Venue: Maine Road

Attendance: 43,246

Division One, 3rd February 1990

Manchester United 1   **Manchester City 1**

Blackmore   Brightwell
Venue: Old Trafford
Attendance: 40,274

1990/91

Division One, 27th October 1990
Manchester City 3   **Manchester United 3**
White (2)   Hughes
Hendry   McClair (2)
Venue: Maine Road
Attendance: 36,427

Division One, 4th May 1991
Manchester United 1   **Manchester City 0**
Giggs
Venue: Old Trafford
Attendance: 45,286

1991/92

Division One, 16th November 1991
Manchester City 0   **Manchester United 0**
Venue: Maine Road
Attendance: 38,180

Division One, 7th April 1992
Manchester United 1   **Manchester City 1**
Giggs   Curle (pen)
Venue: Old Trafford
Attendance: 46,781

1992/93

Premier League, 6th December 1992

Manchester United 2 **Manchester City 1**

Ince   Quinn

Hughes

Venue: Old Trafford

Attendance: 35,408

Premier League, 20th March 1993

Manchester City 1 **Manchester United 1**

Quinn   Cantona

Venue: Maine Road

Attendance: 37,136

1993/94

Premier League, 7th November 1993

Manchester City 2 **Manchester United 3**

Quinn (2)   Cantona (2)

          Keane

Venue: Maine Road

Attendance: 35,155

Premier League, 23rd April 1994

Manchester United 2 **Manchester City 0**

Cantona (2)

Venue: Old Trafford

Attendance: 44,333

1994/95

Premier League, 10th November 1994

Manchester United 5 **Manchester City 0**

Cantona

Kanchelskis (3)

Hughes

Venue: Old Trafford

Attendance: 43,738

Premier League, 11th February 1995

Manchester City 0   **Manchester United 3**

Ince

Kanchelskis

Cole

Venue: Maine Road

Attendance: 26,368

1995/96

Premier League, 14th October 1995

Manchester United 1   **Manchester City 0**

Scholes

Venue: Old Trafford

Attendance: 35,707

FA Cup Fifth Round, 18th February 1996

Manchester United 2   **Manchester City 1**

Cantona (pen)   Rosler

Sharpe

Venue: Old Trafford

Attendance: 42,692

Premier League, 6th April 1996

Manchester City 2   **Manchester United 3**

Kavelashvili   Cantona (pen)

Rosler   Cole

                                Giggs

Venue: Maine Road
Attendance: 29,688

1996/97

No game

1997/98

No game

1998/99

No game

1999/2000

No game

2000/01

Premier League, 18th November 2000

Manchester City 0　　　　**Manchester United 1**

　　　　　　　　　　　　　Beckham

Venue: Maine Road
Attendance: 34,429

Premier League, 21st April 2001

Manchester United 1　　　**Manchester City 1**

Sheringham (pen) Howey
Venue: Old Trafford
Attendance: 67,535

2001/02

No game

2002/03

Premier League, 9th November 2002

Manchester City 3   **Manchester United 1**

Goater (2)   Solskjaer

Anelka

Venue: Maine Road

Attendance: 34,649

Premier League, 9th February 2003

Manchester United 1   **Manchester City 1**

Van Nistelrooy   Goater

Venue: Old Trafford

Attendance: 67,646

2003/04

Premier League, 13th December 2003

Manchester United 3   **Manchester City 1**

Scholes (2)   Wright-Phillips

Van Nistelrooy

Venue: Old Trafford

Attendance: 67,645

FA Cup Fifth Round, 14th February 2004

Manchester United 4   **Manchester City 2**

Scholes   Tarnat

Van Nistelrooy (2)   Fowler

Ronaldo

Venue: Old Trafford

Attendance: 67,228

Premier League, 14th March 2004

Manchester City 4   **Manchester United 1**

Fowler	Scholes
Macken	
Sinclair	
Wright-Phillips	

Venue: City of Manchester Stadium
Attendance: 47,284

2004/05

Premier League, 7th November 2004

Manchester United 0   **Manchester City 0**

Venue: Old Trafford
Attendance: 67,863

Premier League, 13th February 2005

Manchester City 0   **Manchester United 2**

Dunne (o.g.)

Rooney

Venue: City of Manchester Stadium
Attendance: 47,111

2005/06

Premier League, 10th September 2005

Manchester United 1   **Manchester City 1**

Van Nistelrooy   Barton

Venue: Old Trafford
Attendance: 67,839

Premier League, 14th January 2006

Manchester City 3   **Manchester United 1**

Sinclair   Van Nistelrooy

Vassell

Fowler

Venue: City of Manchester Stadium
Attendance: 47,192

2006/07

Premier League, 9th December 2006

Manchester United 3   **Manchester City 1**

Rooney   Trabelsi

Saha

Ronaldo

Venue: Old Trafford
Attendance: 75,858

Premier League, 5th May 2007

Manchester City 0   **Manchester United 1**

                                          Ronaldo (pen)

Venue: City of Manchester Stadium
Attendance: 47,244

2007/08

Premier League, 19th August 2007

Manchester City 1   **Manchester United 0**

Geovanni

Venue: City of Manchester Stadium
Attendance: 44,955

Premier League, 10th February 2008

Manchester United 1   **Manchester City 2**

Carrick   Vassell

                                          Benjani

Venue: Old Trafford
Attendance: 75,970

2008/09

Premier League, 30th November 2008

Manchester City 0   **Manchester United 1**

Rooney

Venue: City of Manchester Stadium
Attendance: 47,320

Premier League, 10th May 2009

Manchester United 2   **Manchester City 0**

Ronaldo

Tevez

Venue: Old Trafford
Attendance: 75,464

2009/10

Premier League, 20th September 2009

Manchester United 4   **Manchester City 3**

Rooney   Barry

Fletcher (2)   Bellamy (2)

Owen

Venue: Old Trafford
Attendance: 75,066

Carling Cup Semi-final (first leg), 19th January 2010

Manchester City 2   **Manchester United 1**

Tevez (2, 1 pen)   Giggs

Venue: City of Manchester Stadium
Attendance: 46,067

Carling Cup Semi-final (second leg), 27th January 2010

Manchester United 3   **Manchester City 1**

Scholes   Tevez

Carrick
Rooney
Venue: Old Trafford
Attendance: 74,576

Premier League, 4th May 2010
Manchester City 0   **Manchester United 1**
                             Scholes
Venue: City of Manchester Stadium
Attendance: 47,320

2010/11

Premier League, 10th November 2010
Manchester City 0   **Manchester United 0**
Venue: City of Manchester Stadium
Attendance: 47,210

Premier League, 12th February 2011
Manchester United 2   **Manchester City 1**
Nani   Silva
Rooney
Venue: Old Trafford
Attendance: 75,322

FA Cup, Semi-final, 16th April 2011
Manchester City 1   **Manchester United 0**
Yaya Touré
Venue: Wembley
Attendance: 86,549

2011/12

FA Community Shield, 7th August 2011

Manchester City 2   **Manchester United 3**

Lescott   Smalling

Dzeko   Nani (2)

Venue: Wembley

Attendance: 77,169

Premier League, 23rd October 2011

Manchester United 1   **Manchester City 6**

Fletcher   Balotelli (2)

     Aguero

     Dzeko (2)

     Silva

Venue: Old Trafford

Attendance: 75,487

FA Cup Third Round, 8th January 2012

Manchester City 2   **Manchester United 3**

Kolarov   Rooney (2, 1 pen)

Aguero   Welbeck

Venue: Etihad Stadium

Attendance: 46,808

Premier League, 30th April 2012

Manchester City 1   **Manchester United 0**

Kompany

Venue: Etihad Stadium

Attendance: 47,219

Facts, Trivia, Records and Profiles

Derby Trivia

Manchester derby records:

- The heaviest peacetime home loss City have suffered against United has been 0-3 on three separate occasions: 10th February 1979, 14th September 1985 and 11th February 1995. Newton Heath also took away a victory by three goals from Hyde Road on 3rd November 1894 as they ran out 5-2 winners. 1994/95 was not a good season for the Blues as they also fell to their heaviest loss at Old Trafford when they went down 5-0 on 10th November.

- Maine Road welcomed 78,000 through the doors on 20th September 1947 to watch the teams play out a 0-0 draw in what remains the highest recorded attendance for a derby played at either side's ground.

- The Blues fared better, with the highest Old Trafford attendance of 75,970 running out 2-1 winners at Old Trafford on 10th February 2008. Goals from Benjani and Darius Vassell, in a match marking the 50th anniversary of the Munich air disaster, sealed the club's first league double over the Reds since 1969/70.

- The early-to-mid Nineties saw the lowest attendances, with only

26,368 attending the 3-0 victory for United at Maine Road on 11th February 1995, while just 35,408 saw the Blues go down 2-1 at Old Trafford on 6th December 1992.

Most derby goals:

Joe Hayes currently sits joint-top of the goal-scoring charts against United. The striker hit 10 goals between 1955 and 1961 – the Blues winning five of the derbies he scored in, drawing twice and only losing once.

Francis Lee equalled Hayes' record shortly afterwards, scoring 10 times in seven games between 1968 and 1972 – including the winner in the League Cup semi-final first leg on 3rd December 1969.

Top all-time derby goal-scorers:

Player	Club	Goals
Joe Hayes	Manchester City	10
Francis Lee	Manchester City	10
Bobby Charlton	Manchester United	9
Colin Bell	Manchester City	8
Eric Cantona	Manchester United	8
Brian Kidd	United & City	8
Wayne Rooney	Manchester United	8
Joe Spence	Manchester United	8
Paul Scholes	Manchester United	7
Dennis Viollet	Manchester United	7

Cup Competitions:

• The teams have met sporadically in the FA Cup and, up until the controversial 2011/12 victory for United, the Blues had won every meeting away from Old Trafford. United have won all four games at their home ground, while Newton Heath also won the first FA Cup encounter in 1891.

- At neutral venues City have progressed to the final twice. On 27th March 1926 a brace from Tommy Browell and a goal from Frank Roberts sent the Blues to Wembley at Sheffield United's Bramall Lane, while a more recent meeting will still be fresh in the mind – Yaya Touré powering past the United defence to send City on their way to FA Cup glory with a 1-0 victory at Wembley. A massive Maine Road crowd of 74,723 saw Joe Hayes and Don Revie dispatch United in 1955.

- City triumphed over United on the way to becoming the League Cup champions in 1970. The Reds were beaten in the semi-finals as Colin Bell and Francis Lee gave the Blues a 2-1 lead from the first leg at Maine Road on 3rd December 1969. A 2-2 draw at Old Trafford on 17th December was enough to see City progress to the final where they would go on to beat West Bromwich Albion and lift the trophy.

- Recently the clubs clashed yet again in the 2009-10 semi-finals. A 2-1 home victory in the first leg on 19th January was not enough to see the Blues through, as United ran out 3-1 winners at Old Trafford eight days later.

- United currently hold the upper hand in the Charity Shield having beaten the Blues on both occasions the sides have met. A modest crowd of 30,495 watched the Reds win 1-0 at Maine Road on 24th October 1956, while in 2011 City contrived to blow a two-goal lead as United triumphed 3-2 in front of a 77,169 crowd at Wembley.

Played for one, managed the other:
Mark Hughes (played for United, managed City)
Manchester United: 1983–86 & 1988–95
Manchester City manager: 2008–2009

United playing record:	Apps	Goals
League	345	120
FA Cup	46	17
League Cup	38	16
Europe	33	9
Other	5	1
Total	467	163

City managerial record:

Games: 67

Wins: 36

Draws: 15

Losses: 16

One of only two men to have played for the Reds and managed the Blues (the other being Steve Coppell), Mark Hughes holds a unique place in Manchester derby history. A firm favourite with the Old Trafford fans, Hughes enjoyed two spells at the club after leaving school in the summer of 1980. "Sparky", as he was affectionately nicknamed, scored on his United debut in November 1983 and helped his side to the 1985 FA Cup with a 1-0 victory over Everton. Hughes was surprisingly sold to Barcelona the following year but was unable to settle at the Nou Camp and was loaned out to Bayern Munich before being brought back to Old Trafford for a fee of £1.5 million by Alex Ferguson in the summer of 1988. His goals helped United steer clear of the possibility of relegation in 1989/90, when they finished just five points clear of the drop zone, and went on to unprecedented success in the 1990s. He was an integral member of the team that won back-to-back league titles between 1992 and 1994, two FA Cups (1990 and 1994), a League Cup (1992) and a European Cup Winners' Cup (1991), before leaving Old Trafford for a second time in July 1995. A Welsh international, with 72 caps and 16 goals, Hughes went on to win further trophies with Chelsea (including the 1997 FA Cup) and Blackburn Rovers before retiring in July 2002. He then moved into management, taking on the Wales and Blackburn Rovers managerial positions before moving to City in June 2008. He spent 18 months with the Blues and was in charge of three Manchester derbies but his team lost them all.

Played for United once, City twice:
Denis Law
Manchester City: 1960–61 & 1973–74
Manchester United: 1962–73

Born: 24th February 1940
Birthplace: Aberdeen, Scotland
Position: Centre-forward

United record:	Apps	Goals
League	309	171
FA Cup	46	34
League Cup	11	3
Europe	33	28
Other	5	1
Total	404	237

City record:	Apps	Goal
League	68	30
FA Cup	5	4
League Cup	6	3
Europe	-	-
Other	-	-
Total	79	37

Second only to Bobby Charlton in United's goal-scorers list, Denis Law proved a revelation on his return from Italy in July 1962 for a new British record fee of £115,000. His professional career had begun at Huddersfield Town, but Law also played for Manchester City and Torino before his arrival at Old Trafford where his predatory instinct led him to average a goal in less than two games. He helped United to the FA Cup in his first season – scoring his side's first goal in the 3-1 victory over Leicester City – and went on to win two league titles before the decade was out. Ironically, he missed out on the 1968 European Cup final with a knee injury; it was this problem that would hamper his final few years at Old Trafford. He was allowed to leave on a free transfer in the summer of 1973 and saw out his final season as a professional with Manchester City, and scored the goal that condemned the Reds to the second division – it was his last kick in club football. Law scored 30 times in 55 games for his country and was a member of the Scotland squad that remained undefeated at the 1974 World Cup.

Played for United once, City twice: Billy Meredith
Manchester City: 1894–1907 & 1921–24
Manchester United: 1907–21

Born: 30th July 1874
Birthplace: Chirk, Wales
Died: 19th April 1958
Position: Forward

City record:	Apps	Goal
League	366	145
FA Cup	23	5
Other	4	1
Total	393	151

United record:	Apps	Goals
League	303	35
FA Cup	29	0
Other	3	1
Total	335	36

Commonly considered the first superstar of English league football, Billy Meredith was the first City captain to lift the FA Cup trophy.

The "Welsh Wizard" was an instrumental figure in the club's earliest years and, only five years on from the club's inception, in 1894, he helped his side reach the top tier of English football by winning the Division Two Championship in 1899.

Despite suffering relegation three years later Meredith helped the Blues secure an automatic return to Division One the following season and continued to win the adoration of fans across the country with his exciting style of play.

In 1904 the player, famous for chewing on a toothpick during games, led his side out in their first FA Cup final. The captain led by example by putting in a man-of-the-match performance and his 23rd-minute strike proved the only goal of the game as the Blues beat Bolton 1-0 to become the first Manchester side to win a major trophy. In fact, Meredith's side were unlucky not to complete a league and cup double that season as City finished runners-up, just three points off the Division One summit.

After finding himself caught up in a bribery scandal in 1906, Meredith moved across the city to join United – where he would win the FA Cup again in 1909 – before returning to the Blue half of Manchester in 1921.

The iconic forward spent three years at City during his second spell at the club and became the oldest player to ever appear in the FA Cup.

Not only have Meredith's achievements been recognized by City, but in 2007 he was inducted into English football's Hall of Fame alongside World Cup winner Nobby Stiles and former City manager Mark Hughes.

In an even more fitting tribute – one which truly reflected Meredith's influence on the game – the Professional Footballers' Association combined with the Welsh FA and both Manchester clubs to fund a headstone for the grave of the City and United legend who had died in 1958.

Played for both: Peter Schmeichel

Manchester United: 1991–99
Manchester City: 2002–03

Born: 18th November 1963
Birthplace: Gladsaxe, Denmark
Position: Goalkeeper

United record:	Apps	Goals
League	292	0
FA Cup	41	0
League Cup	17	0
Europe	42	1
Other	6	0
Total	398	1

City record:	Apps	Goal
League	29	0
FA Cup	1	0
League Cup	1	0
Europe	-	-
Other	-	-
Total	31	0

When Peter Schmeichel arrived at Old Trafford from Brondby for £500,000 in August 1991, the fans had little idea what to expect. A commanding keeper, with great shot-stopping skills and the ability to make himself a big target for incoming attackers to evade, Schmeichel was the backbone of United during the 1990s and helped his side to five league titles, three FA Cups, one League Cup and a Champions League final that proved to be his United swansong. He moved to Portugal with Sporting CP before returning to play for Aston Villa and then City, where he was part of a side that beat the Reds 3-1 at Maine Road and drew 1-1 at Old Trafford. He retired after just one season with the Blues.

Ernest Mangnall:

Ernest Mangnall is the only man to have managed both clubs. He oversaw United's first national trophy wins, gaining two league titles and one FA Cup. In September 1912 Mangnall agreed to join City but remained in charge of United for two more games. His final match in charge of United was a derby which his new employers, City, won 1-0. He signed Billy Meredith for United from City in 1906 and did the same again in 1921, but in the opposite direction. Off the field he played an important role in both United's move to Old Trafford in 1910 and City's move to Maine Road in 1923.

Finally, two former stalwarts of the Manchester derby sum up what this fixture really means to the players...

Derby Day memories: Mike Doyle, Manchester City (*Courtesy Manchester Evening News*)

Former City skipper Mike Doyle has one of the best Manchester derby records of any player. Doyle clocked up 558 appearances for his boyhood heroes over a 16-year period and there was a time when United just couldn't handle City as they beat the Reds – comfortably – time and time again. Many believe it was Doyle's legendary hatred of the Old Trafford club that drove the Blues on to dominate the fixture between March 1968 and September 1975.

Doyle played in 16 derby games and was on the losing side just once in that amazing seven-year period when the Blue half of Manchester enjoyed a similar stronghold over their neighbours that United would enjoy during the mid-1990s until 2012.

The build-up to the derby would invariably see Doyle interviewed in the Press, radio or television. Journalists knew they'd always get a good line from the man United fans loved to hate as he stoked the pre-match fires up to fever pitch with his boasts about what City were going to do.

Indeed, he often dismissed the Reds as "four easy points" and admitted he was gutted when they were relegated in 1974 because it was the loss of two guaranteed victories!

The comments – hardly surprisingly – didn't go down too well with United supporters and Doyle became the target of hate mail, vandalism and even death threats. The police took one caller so seriously they even gave Doyle round-the-clock protection throughout the week leading up to a clash at Old Trafford. Typically, Doyle refused to pull out of the match and, though the perpetrator was never caught, he took the threats with a pinch of salt. He played and City won the game.

Many wondered exactly why he hated United so much and, though he admits to have never been particularly enamoured by the Old Trafford club, he says the press coverage of the time had something to do with it.

"I remember where it really all began," recalled Doyle in 2008. "We were returning home from Belgium after a match in the European Cup Winners' Cup and were the last British club in Europe. But when we got the early editions of the English papers we were given a small paragraph on an inside page.

"The headlines on the back were about United, who weren't doing particularly well at that time. They had won a meaningless testimonial or friendly match and the headlines were something along the lines of 'Reds Roar Back'.

"Both Mike Summerbee and myself were livid and told the journalists on the plane exactly what we thought. One reporter asked why didn't I express my views in an interview. So I did and the next day the headline was: 'Doyle Hates United!' That was it as far as journalists were concerned. When a clash with United was imminent they came looking for me and, to be honest, I enjoyed winding the Reds' fans up."

City's domination in the games was total and Doyle's favourite moment was scoring a soaring header at the Stretford End to give City a 4-1 win. But there were so many happy moments, it is not easy for him to pick just one.

"People used to say I hated United, but it was more of a dislike," he said. "They used to get so much coverage at a time they weren't a good side that it used to rile me and the rest of the lads. We were winning everything in sight but we never got the credit we deserved."

Doyle also received his marching orders in one derby game when he and Lou Macari were given an early bath for a harmless clash on the halfway line. Both players refused to leave the field so referee, Clive Thomas, took all 22 players off! He wouldn't restart the game until Doyle and Macari accepted they were going to play no further part in the match.

There was one incident that Doyle will never forget from an Old Trafford derby and, for a moment, it looked like he was ready to throttle the mercurial Irishman who had scythed down his best pal, Glyn Pardoe, in a horrific challenge.

"I remember the incident vividly," recalled Doyle. "The tackle George [Best] made on Glyn was terrible. He went over the ball and launched Glyn up in the air and broke his leg.

"I got hold of Best by the throat and Brian Kidd and Tony Book had to pull me off him because I was so furious. George ended up being substituted after I tackled him three times in quick succession as I sought retribution within the laws of the game.

"They rushed Glyn to the MRI and, had it not been for the actions of Sydney Rose, he may have had to have had his leg amputated from the ankle down. Thankfully, he was okay but the tackle effectively finished his career."

Doyle, who sadly passed away in 2010, remained a staunch Blue until the day he died. He summed the lot of a City fan perfectly when he once said: "I'm always optimistic with City but I'd never back them. They are a bookies nightmare!"

Derby Day memories: Lou Macari, Manchester United (*Courtesy Manchester Evening News*)

Lou Macari will never forget the 1974 Maine Road derby. The police were called into Manchester United's dressing room to stop him playing – it's a long story...

Macari clashed with the Blues' Mike Doyle and both refused to leave the pitch after being sent off.

Despite Macari and Doyle's on-field spat they were in total agreement that controversial referee Clive Thomas had gone over the top.

United were fighting First Division relegation at the time, while the Blues were parading expensive new debutants Dennis Tueart and Micky Horswill. The local dust-up boiled over early on when Doyle floored Macari.

"It was a bit different from these days where players tend to either stay down or roll about," recalled Macari.

"I hit the deck after Mike Doyle, surprise, surprise, chopped me down. That was one of the most predictable things about derbies in those days that Mike would chop you down!

"I bounced straight back up again and threw the ball in his direction. It hit him on the shoulder or the side of his ear.

"The referee Clive 'the Book' Thomas certainly lived up to his nickname. If it hadn't been him in charge then we'd have expected to have had a word with the ref and then get a booking each. But with Clive you partly feared the sending off. Thomas lived up to his reputation and sent us both packing.

"It was only a trip from Mike, and mine was only a minor retaliation. It was what you'd expect in those days following an incident like that in a derby. It was a bit dramatic of Clive but that went hand in hand with him.

"Both of us thought he was a bit hasty and over the top on both counts. You used to give someone a push and a shove in those days to let them know they weren't going to mess you around.

"But Clive was of the opinion that we weren't going to mess him around. We had a chat for two or three minutes on the pitch but Mike and I simply refused to go. In the end he had no alternative but to take everybody off.

"Clive ordered us all off to the dressing rooms. After a break he appeared in our room with two policemen, pointed to me and said: 'He's not to go back out again.'

"Thomas then went into City's changing room and did the same with Mike Doyle! Our little protest was over and we had to have the proverbial early bath.

"Once the two flair players had gone off what chance had the game got, and it ended 0-0."

Acknowledgements

No book is constructed by the work of one single person. There are many who contribute, either directly or indirectly, and, whichever the case may be, I am indebted to a number of people.

Firstly, thanks to Richard Havers and Jeremy Yates-Round at Haynes for commissioning this book, and a big thanks to Becky Ellis for weeding out inaccuracies and suggesting intelligent additions and omissions. Thanks also to David Scripps at Mirrorpix for all his help and advice regarding the *Daily Mirror* archive of which many facts and figures have been sourced. I am also deeply indebted to Gary James and Steve Cawley for their fantastic archive book *The Pride of Manchester,* which really helped me get a feel for the early encounters via some of their meticulously researched text. Now you've bought this book, I can heartily recommend you seek out that, too! Also, a big thanks to Michael Heatley and Ian Welch's book *The Great Derby Matches*, which also led me down one or two fascinating paths. Ian also helped me with one or two player profiles as the deadline rapidly approached so, again, I'm hugely grateful for his assistance.

Thanks also to Daniel Morehead.

Thanks to all the unnamed journalists who wrote match reports and discovered little-known facts along the way, particularly the guys who were writing about this game long before I, my parents and grandparents were born. You may be too numerous to list, but thanks to each and every one of you.

To my family, as per usual, thanks for allowing me the time to write this. The precious hours I lose writing can never be fully replaced, but I will try, I promise.

Last of all, a big thanks to the City and United fans, and to the players of both clubs who have taken part in each and every Manchester derby – from the very first to the most recent – and made it the match that it is.

Others may disagree, but this is still the best derby in world football. Red and Blue, City and United – there's no game that even comes close...